THE BEST ML JOKES

BY BRUNO KASSEL AND CARLO MAY

MORE THAN 500 JOKES

No part of this publication, such as the music, text, design and graphics, may be reproduced in any form or by any means without the prior written permission of the publishers.

Cover illustration by Michael Schmitt
Other illustrations by Justo G. Pulido
Layout by B & O

Voggenreiter Publishers
Viktoriastr. 25, 53173 Bonn/Germany
www.voggenreiter.de
info@voggenreiter.de

ISBN: 3-8024-0368-1

Contents

Foreword
by Pete York

Laughter is very important to musicians. You have to laugh about a career in which the more you learn to master your instrument the less likely you are to make a living playing it.

We are bombarded every day by the media showing us that the way to success in music is to come up with a childishly simple song with as little melody and harmony as possible, a deafening machine-generated beat and a thoroughly tasteless and negative lyric sung out of tune. This must be performed whilst jerking and writhing as if recently bitten by a sea-snake. Any languid and genuinely erotic movement will upset your target audience who are aged eight and a half.

You may wear baggy clothing or scraps of leather, plastic, latex or, best of all, rubber. Any combination of these will appeal to the kiddies who have only just left the toilet-training stages of life and fondly remember diapers and other garments of containment.

The revealing of large areas of naked flesh will also increase your chances, especially if the skin is wet or oily. This will remind your viewers/listeners of the occasional failure of the aforementioned garments.

So, my dear striving musician friends, follow my advice, make millions and retire to Paradise Island before your twenty-first birthday.

Except you won't. Hopefully you'll laugh at the above example of cynical humor and go back to enjoying your instrument. Ignore the dross that MTV churns out and search for the best in MUSIC. Along the way you'll find the best in humor too because musicians love to laugh about themselves. And that's the reason for this delightful little book.

I would strongly advise every performing player to keep a copy close-by because, if the power goes off, a string breaks, a lip splits, a drum stick cracks or the soprano swallows her false teeth, you can become a stand-up comedian for a few minutes until the show can go on.

That's what I do anyway...

Some of the most amusing lines come out of real life situations. At least I hope they're true, because they are so delicious. Here's how I heard them anyway.

Highly experienced session singer, Lee Gibson, is sitting in an empty recording studio ready to begin her work. The Spice Girls march in and are outraged to see her sitting there.

SPICE GIRLS (in dodgy harmony): "What do you think you're doing in here? This studio is booked for us. And who are you anyway?"

LEE: "...I'm your voice!"

Eric Clapton had decided to change his band and summoned them all to explain his reasons, i.e. that the Eric Clapton Band as it had been known for several years would be no more. The excellent drummer was the good-humored, Steve Ferrone.

STEVE: "That's fine, Eric, but can we keep the name?"

A fine group of English session guys have turned up to put down some tracks with Bob Dylan in a London studio, among them the tremendously experienced Scottish guitar giant, Jim Mullen. There is no sign of Bob. Hours go by and the great man fails to appear. The musicians are becoming restless to say the least. Finally, an American manager steps in to address the band, who have waited all day.

AMERICAN MANAGER: "Bob won't be coming in today. He's got problems with his voice."

JIM: "What voice???"

Another story of life on the road with Buddy Rich, as told to me by the one and only Jake Hanna, although the Rotten Kid is only the audience here. The Buddy Rich Sextet has a new piano player and he is in the middle of an exploratory solo, maybe too much Cecil Taylor and not enough Art Tatum. The old-pro sax player takes out his linen handkerchief, opens it and spreads it over the pianist's furiously working fingers.

PIANIST: "What did you do that for?"

SAX: "I'm covering up the scene of the crime."

PIANIST: "You should be careful how you talk to me. I used to be a boxer."

SAX: "Then maybe you should have taken your gloves off before you came to the gig."

Buddy fell off his seat with laughter. He loved it when others could be as acidly funny as he was.

Keith Richards, the man who put the stone into Rolling, had invited his father to Paris to see one of their concerts. After the show, the entourage made their various ways back to the hotel. Charlie Watts discovered Mr. Richards senior already at the bar enjoying a large cognac.

CHARLIE: "You should take it easy with that stuff, Mr. Richards, or one day you'll look like your son!"

Now these tales and many others have been passed around amongst the musos and we delight in them because they deal with names we all know, and they're funny.

They are also a tribute to those names who can both dish out a comic comment or be on the receiving end. There is no cruelty here and it seems healthy to be able to kid around with one another; something that musicians do a lot. I love the drummer jokes and they do have a ring of truth about them.

Whatever instrument you play, I want to wish you a happy and satisfying life doing something you love: making music – how lucky we are. Yes, we certainly need a sense of humor, and you'll find a lot of it here in THE BEST MUSICIANS' JOKES!

Pete York

[played with The Spencer Davis Group feat. Steve Winwood (Number One-Hits: "Keep On Running", "Gimme Some Lovin' ", "I'm A Man"), with Hardin & York ("the World's Smallest Big Band"), with Jon Lord ("Rock Meets Classic"), wrote and performed in the TV series "Super Drumming" with the cream of the world's drummers (Louie Bellson, Cozy Powell, Ian Paice, Simon Phillips, Gerry Brown, Billy Cobham, Nicko McBrain, Zak Starkey, Dave Mattacks, Bill Bruford, Ed Thigpen, Mark Brzezicki, Steve Ferrone, Jon Hiseman etc.), played tribute concerts to Gene Krupa, George Gershwin and Duke Ellington]

Introduction

There are jokes about lawyers, doctors, psychiatrists and golfers, and also jokes about blondes. There are tons of jokes. But are there any jokes about musicians? Some say, absolutely not! Everything you hear and say about them is true, no getting around it. Are we really able to make fun of the musician, this very special species of the terrestrial fauna? The complexity of his personality is best described by a simple comparison:

How to impress a woman

Compliment her,
cuddle her,
kiss her,
caress her,
love her,
tease her,
comfort her,
protect her,
hug her,
hold her,
spend money on her,
wine & dine her,
buy things for her,
listen to her,
care for her,
stand by her,
support her,
go to the ends of the earth
for her.

How to impress a musician

Show up naked.
Bring beer.

For years, the authors tried hard to study musicians all over the planet. Their results and their experiences have been written down in this book. It's an attempt to show the world some of those who live among us, as long as there still remains no cure for this unique life form (drum roll, please): the musician.

Bruno and Carlo would like to thank Marion Stroemer, the Jule Neigel Band, Simon Phillips & Toto, Marco Minnemann, Dom Famularo, the one and only Buddy Rich, Pete York, Dieter Geis, Vocaleros, Fury In The Slaughterhouse, Harald Schmidt, David Letterman, Carola Grey, Torsten de Winkel, Nick Vinzentz, Rick Abao, Steve "Snoopy" Allen, Jule Njankouo, Dennis "Az Hosers" Dennison, Bertram Engel, Achim Faerber, Gero Zahn, Iris Hilker, Attila Kormanyos, Meike Koester, Tanja Krueger, Glen Mansell, Axel Mikolajczak, Dieter Roesberg, David Qualey, Miriam Pielhau, Robert Lyng, Pete Townshend, Gabi Lang, Stefan Weinand, Gina and Adam Schairer of Naples/Florida, the O'Five guys Michael Kiesewetter & Joerg Petersen of Cape Coral/Florida and Seth Josel for his help with da werdz, Charles & Ralph Voggenreiter, and all of our readers in Germany over the past few years.

If you have any questions or more musicians' jokes for the next edition of this book, feel free to contact me/us under **www.BrunoKassel.de** or e-mail me/us at **BK@BrunoKassel.de** – your feedback is always welcome!

Cologne/Germany, August 2001

Homo Musicus
(aka: the musician)

What do you call a good looking, intelligent, sensible musician who plays perfectly?

A rumor.

One day, an out-of-work musician is visiting the zoo and attempts to earn some money as a street performer. Unfortunately, as soon as he starts to draw a crowd, a zoo-keeper grabs him and drags him into his office.

The zoo-keeper explains to the musician that the zoo's most popular attraction, a gorilla, has died suddenly and the keeper fears that attendance at the zoo will drop. He offers the musician a job to dress up as the gorilla until they can get another one. The musician accepts.

So, the next morning the musician puts on the gorilla suit and enters the cage before the crowd comes. He discovers that it's a great job. He can sleep all he wants, play and make fun of people, and he draws bigger crowds than he ever did as a musician.

However,.eventually the crowds tire of him and he tires of just swinging on tires. He begins to notice that the people are paying more attention to the lion in the cage next to his.

Not wanting to lose the attention of his audience, he climbs onto the top of his cage, crawls across a partition, and dangles from the top onto the lion's cage. Of course, this makes the lion furious, but the crowd loves it.

At the end of the day, the zoo-keeper comes and gives the musician a raise for being as good an attraction as the gorilla.

Well, this goes on for some time, the musician keeps taunting the lion, the crowds grow larger, and his salary keeps going up. Then, one terrible day when he is dangling over the furious lion, he slips and falls. The musician is terrified. The lion gathers itself and prepares to pounce. The musician is so scared that he begins to run round and round the cage with the lion close behind.

Finally, the musician starts screaming and yelling, "Help me, Help me!", but the lion is quick and pounces.

The musician soon finds himself flat on his back looking up at the angry lion and the lion says, "Shut up you idiot! Do you want to get us both fired?"

Two jazz musicians meet passing on the street one day. But one looks forlorn, and almost on the verge of tears. His friend asks, "What has the world done to you, my old friend?"

The sad fellow says, "Let me tell you. Three weeks ago, an uncle died and left me forty thousand dollars."

"That's not bad."

"But you see, two weeks ago, a cousin I never even knew kicked the bucket, and left me eighty-five thousand free and clear."

"Sounds like you should be grateful..."

"You don't understand!" he interrupted. "Last week my great-aunt passed away. I inherited almost a quarter of a million."

Now he was really confused. "Then, how come you look so glum?"

"This week ... nothing!"

Researchers wanted to determine whether dogs took on the characteristics of their masters. So they set up an experiment in their lab with three dog owners and their dogs. The first owner was a mathematician, the second a chemist, the third a musician! The first dog, owned by the mathematician, was quite impressive and, when thrown a bunch of milk bones onto the floor, used her paws to begin arranging them into elaborate mathematical equations! "Pretty good!" said the researchers, "but not conclusive!" The second dog, owned by the chemist, when thrown a bunch of milk bones on the floor, began to arrange them to display complex chemical formulas! "Not bad!" said the researchers, "but still not conclusive enough!" However, the results of the third dog WERE very convincing in proving that dogs DO take on the characteristics of their owners: The musician's dog came late, ate all the bones, then left early!

What has 100 legs and four teeth?
The front row at a Mississippi Bluegrass festival.

How do you tell you are at a Bluegrass show?
If there are more people on the stage than in the audience.

What does new age music sound like played backwards?
New age music.

What happens when you play "the blues" backwards?
Your wife comes back to you, your dog returns to life, you get out of prison and you get your job back.

Why are music critics' columns bad choices to line the bottom of a bird cage?
It's too hard to distinguish the droppings from the writing.

What do you get if you cross a music critic with a bowling ball?
A bowling ball that wouldn't know a good performance if it heard one.

What do you get if you cross a music critic with a music critic?
A bad review.

What is the definition of a Soviet string quartet?
A Soviet symphony orchestra after a tour of the USA!

Why did the Philharmonic disband?
Excessive sax and violins.

What takes up the most space on a sheet of rock music?
All the fs for fortissimo-issimo...-issimos.

Why didn't the music students get to learn music in 1999?
Because 1998 the music.

So, anyway, there's this jazz trumpet player who's never made the money he wanted, but hey, that's jazz. He gets run over by a bus and due to his unruly life, goes down to Hell. He stands at the rusty iron gates when a bellowing voice calls out, "Jazz musician are we?..............corridor C, door 14!" So on he treks, trumpet firmly in hand. As he walks down the corridor, he's struck dumb by this absolutely amazing jazz jam going on. He follows the sound, picking up speed until he finally comes to the source of the "Heavenly" sound..........door 14. He can't believe his luck when he opens the door, Dizzy Gillespie, Miles Davis, Buddy Rich..........all the Greats are here. Dizzy looks over at him and says, "Pull up a pew son and let the jazz free". He starts playing, still dumb-founded with his luck. If this is Hell, then he'll happily spend eternity here. Just then, the door opens and in walks the Devil: "'Right boys and girls, break time over!......a-one-two-three-four, 'Left a good job in the city.....'."

On the way from one venue to the next, a truck driver from a well-known heavy metal band stopped at a roadside diner for lunch, and ordered a cheeseburger, coffee, and a slice of apple pie. As he was about to eat, three motorcycles pulled up outside. The bikers came in, and one grabbed the trucker's cheeseburger out of his hand and took a huge bite from it. The second one drank the trucker's coffee, and the third wolfed down his apple pie.

The truck driver didn't say a word. He simply got up, paid the cashier, and left. When he was gone, the other motorcyclists snickered to one another and congratulated each other on being so "bad". As the cashier walked up, one of the motorcyclists growled, "He ain't much of a man, is he?"

"He's not much of a driver, either," the cashier replied. "He just backed his 18-wheeler over three motorcycles."

A groupie went to an appliance store sale and found a bargain. "I would like to buy this TV," she told the salesman. "Sorry, we don't sell to groupies," he replied. She hurried home and dyed her hair, then came back and again told the salesman, "I would like to buy this TV." "Sorry, we don't sell to groupies," he replied. "Darn, he recognized me," she thought. She went for a complete disguise this time, haircut and new color, new outfit, big sunglasses, then waited a few days before she again approached the salesman. "I would like to buy this TV." "Sorry, we don't sell to groupies," he replied. Frustrated, she exclaimed: "How do you know I'm a groupie?" "Because," he replied. "That's a microwave."

A jazz musician was trying to pull out of a parking place, but bashed the bumper of the parked car in front of him. Witnessed by a handful of pedestrians waiting for a bus, the driver got out, inspected the damage, and proceeded to write a note to leave on the windshield of the car he had hit.

The note read: "Hello. I have just hit your car, and there are some people here watching me who think that I am writing this note to leave you my name, phone number, and driver's license number, but I am not."

A jazz musician goes to a bar and yells: "QUICK!!!! Give me a glass of beer!!! Before it gets started!!!" The bartender goes: "What gets started? What are you talking about?" "No questions. Just give me the beer, faster!!!" He drinks the beer and screams again: "One more, hurry up!!! Before it gets started!!!" "What started?" "Never mind!!! Give me my beer!!!" He drinks the second glass and continues: "Third glass!!! Faster!!! before it gets started!!! Do it!!!" Finally, the bartender asks: "Hey, pal. Are you gonna pay???" And the jazz musician goes: "Dang it! It started..."

Two guys are standing on the curb when a taxi pulls up. One is holding a pair of drumsticks, and the other is carrying a guitar. Who is the professional musician?
The taxi driver.

Why is walking down the street like music?
Because if you don't C# you'll Bb.

What is the difference between a musician and a 16 inch Pepperoni pizza?
A 16 inch Pepperoni pizza can feed a family of four.

Generally speaking, how late does a band play?
About one beat behind the drummer.

What does it say on a blues singer's tombstone?
"Well...I didn't wake up this mornin'..."

What's the difference between a puppy and a singer-songwriter?
Eventually the puppy stops whining.

Know how to make a million dollars singing jazz?
Start with two million.

Why was the music theorist drunk?
He tried to use a fifth with his tonic.

Two musicians are driving down a road. All of a sudden they notice the Grim Reaper in the back seat. Death informs them that they have had an accident and they have both died. But, before he must take them off into eternity, he grants each musician one last request to remind them of their past life on earth. The first musician says he was a country & western musician and would like to hear eight choruses of 'Achy-Breaky Heart' as a last hoorah! The second musician says "I was a jazz musician...kill me first!"

A newly graduated doctor gets a job at the morgue. As he is going through the bodies, he discovers a body with a cork in the crack of its butt. After much debate, he decides to take out the cork. When he pulls it out he suddenly hears country music. When he puts it back in, it stops. Puzzled, he goes to his advisor and tells him what happened. The advisor says, "You think that's strange?" "Yes! Don't you?!" replies the young doctor. "Well," said the advisor, "any asshole can play country music."

What do you

...get if you run over an army officer with a steam roller?
A flat major.

...say to an army officer as you're about to run him (or her) over with a steam roller?
Be flat, major.

...say after you run an army officer over with a steam roller?
See flat major.

...get when an army officer puts his nose to the grindstone?
A sharp major.

A jazz musician was told by his doctor, "I am very sorry to tell you that you have cancer and you have only one more year to live."
The jazz musician replied, "And what am I going to live on for an entire year?"

I was playing in a night club, and getting a few requests and small tips. Towards the end of the night, a man walked up with a wad of bills in his hand and asked me to play a jazz chord. I played an Amaj7. He said, "No, no. A jazz chord."
I did a little improvisational thing, but he didn't like that either.
"No, no, no! A jazz chord. You know, 'A jazz chord, to say, ah love you.'"

There were two people walking down the street. One was a musician. The other didn't have any money either.

The stages of a musician's life:
1. Who is *?
2. Get me *!
3. Get me someone who sounds like *.
4. Get me a young *.
5. Who is *?
(* = enter the musician's name of your choice)

What would a musician do if he won a million dollars?
Continue to play gigs until the money ran out.

While proudly showing off his new apartment to friends, a music college student led the way into the den.
"What is the big brass gong and hammer for?" one of his friends asked.
"That is the talking clock," the man replied.
"How's it work?" the friend asked.
"Watch," the music student said, and then proceeded to give the gong an ear-shattering pound with the hammer.
Suddenly someone screamed from the other side of the wall, "KNOCK IT OFF, YOU JERK! IT'S 2 A.M.!"

A community orchestra was plagued by attendance problems. Several musicians were absent at each rehearsal. As a matter of fact, every player in the orchestra had missed several rehearsals, except for one very faithful oboe player. Finally, as the dress rehearsal drew to a close, the conductor took a moment to thank the oboist for her faithful attendance. She, of course, humbly responded, "It's the least I could do, since I won't be at the performance."

St. Peter's still checking ID's. He asks a man, "What did you do on earth?"
The man says, "I was a doctor."
St. Peter says, "Ok, go right through those Pearly Gates. Next! What did you do on earth?"
"I was a school teacher."
"Go right through those Pearly Gates. Next! And what did you do on earth?"
"I was a musician."
"Go around the side, up the freight elevator, through the kitchen..."

Saint Peter is checking ID's at the Pearly Gates, and first comes a Texan. "Tell me, what have you done in life?" says St. Peter.

The Texan says, "Well, I struck oil, so I became rich, but I didn't sit on my laurels – I divided all my money among my entire family in my will, so our descendants are all set for about three generations."

St. Peter says, "That's quite something. Come on in. Next!"

The second guy in line has been listening, so he says, "I struck it big on the stock market, but I didn't selfishly just provide for my own like that Texan guy. I donated five million to Save the Children."

"Wonderful!" says Saint Peter. "Come in. Who's next?"

The third guy has been listening, and says timidly with a downcast look, "Well, I only made five thousand dollars in my entire lifetime."

"Heavens!" says St. Peter. "What instrument did you play?"

A guy walks into the doctor's office and says, "Doc, I haven't had a bowel movement in a week!" The doctor gives him a prescription for a mild laxative and tells him, "If it doesn't work, let me know."

A week later the guy is back: "Doc, still no movement!"

The doctor says, "Hmm, guess you need something stronger," and prescribes a powerful laxative.

Still another week later the poor guy is back: "Doc, STILL nothing!"

The doctor, worried, says, "We'd better get some more information about you to try to figure out what's going on. What do you do for a living?"

"I'm a musician."

The doctor looks up and says, "Well, that's it! Here's $ 10. Go get something to eat!"

𝄞

The symphony orchestra was performing Beethoven's Ninth. In the piece, there's a long passage of about 20 minutes, during which the bass violinists have nothing to do. Rather than sit around that whole time looking stupid, some bassists decided to sneak offstage and go to the tavern next door for a quick one. After slamming several beers in quick succession, one of them looked at his watch and said, "Hey! We need to get back!"

"No need to panic," said a fellow bassist. "I thought we might need some extra time, so I tied the last few pages of the conductor's score together with string. It'll take him a few minutes to get it untangled."

A few moments later, they staggered back to the concert hall and took their places in the orchestra. About this time, a member of the audience noticed that the conductor seemed a bit edgy and said as much to her companion.

"Well, of course," said her companion. "Don't you see? It's the bottom of the Ninth, the score is tied, and the bassists are loaded."

𝄞

When Beethoven passed away, he was buried in a churchyard. A couple days later, the town drunk was walking through the cemetery and heard a strange noise coming from the area where Beethoven was buried. Terrified, the drunk ran and got the priest to come and listen to. The priest bent close to the grave and heard some faint, unrecognizable music coming from it. Frightened, the priest ran and got the town magistrate.

When the magistrate arrived, he bent his ear to the grave, listened for a moment, and said, "Ah, yes, that's Beethoven's Ninth Symphony, being played backwards."

He listened a while longer, and said, "There's the Eighth Symphony, and it's backwards, too. Most puzzling." So the magistrate kept listening, "There's the Seventh... the Sixth... the Fifth..."

Suddenly the realization of what was happening dawned on the magistrate. He stood up and announced to the crowd that had gathered in the cemetery, "My fellow citizens, there's nothing to worry about. It's just Beethoven, he's decomposing."

Beethoven was so profoundly deaf that he thought his whole life through that he was a painter.

Why don't they know where Mozart is buried?
Because he's really Haydn!

Why did Mozart kill his chickens?
Because they always ran around going "Bach! Bach! Bach!"

Kenny G gets on an elevator and says, "Wow! This rocks!"

What's the difference between Kenny G and a machine gun?
The machine gun repeats only 10 times per second.

Guitar

What do a guitar solo and premature ejaculation have in common?
You know it's coming and there's nothing you can do about it.

How do you get two guitar players to play in perfect unison?
Shoot one.

The Pope and a guitar player find themselves together before the Pearly Gates. After passing out their wings, halos, harps, and such, the admitting angel flies them to their new lodgings. First he takes them to a huge palatial estate with all sorts of lavish trappings. This, the angel announces, is where the guitar player will be spending eternity. The Pope thinks to himself, "Boy oh boy! If he's getting a place like this, I can't wait to see what's in store for me!" The angel and the Pope take flight once more, ending up on a mundane street lined with brick row houses. The Pope is shown to the third walk-up on the left, and the angel turns to leave. "Wait a minute!" cries the pontiff. "What's the deal here? You put that guitar player in a beautiful estate and I, a spiritual leader and paragon of virtue, end up with this dive!" The angel replies, "Look here, old fellow, this street is full of spiritual leaders from many times and religions. You guys are a dime a dozen. We put you here together so you can get your dogma together. The other guy got the mansion because he's the first guitar player to ever make it up here!"

How do you make your mom drive really fast?
Put your guitar in the middle of the road.

Three guitarists collaborated on a book of scales. Each contributed the one he knew.

What's the best thing to play on guitar?
Solitaire.

It's the hour before Pentecostal church, and the pastor comes up to the guitar player and says "I'm glad to see you include biblical precepts in your guitar playing." The guitarist asks, "Do you mean 'make a joyful noise unto the Lord, all ye peoples?'" "No", says the pastor. "'Don't let the left hand know what the right hand is doing.'"

What's the difference between a Stratocaster and a Les Paul?
A Stratocaster burns hotter; a Les Paul burns longer.

How can you tell if a guitar player is at your door?
The knocking gets louder.

What are the two most frequent lies told by heavy metal guitarists?
1. I am not too loud!
2. I have already turned the sound down!

How can you tell if you're talking to a good guitarist?
He doesn't claim to be a bad-ass.

What did the guitarist do when he was told to turn on his amp?
He caressed it softly and told it that he loved it.

Why are electric guitarists so bad in bed?
Because they don't have an amplifier there...

What do an electric guitar and a vacuum cleaner have in common?
Both suck when you plug them in.

True or false: A guitar is a transposed instrument.
True: Am7 transposes to A maj, E7(+9) transposes to E maj, Db maj7 b5 transposes to D maj, C#7 b5 (+13) transposes to E maj...etc.

How do you rescue a drowning guitar player?
Throw his amp in the water, too.

How do you get a guitarist to turn the volume down?
Put some sheet music in front of him.

What do you call two guitarists playing in unison?
Counterpoint.

What is the first thing that a lead guitarist does when he wakes up in the morning?
He rolls over and introduces himself.

Bass

At a convention of biologists one researcher remarks to another, "Did you know that in our lab we have switched from mice to bass players for our experiments?"

"Really?" the other replied, "Why did you switch?"

"Well, for three reasons. First, we found that bass players are far more plentiful, second, the lab assistants don't get so attached to them, and third, there are some things even a rat won't do. There is one drawback, however".

"What's that?" "Sometimes it's hard to extrapolate our test results to human beings."

What's the difference between a bass and a trampoline?
You take off your shoes to jump on the trampoline.

How do you make a double bass sound in-tune?
Chop it up and make it into a xylophone.

Why don't bass players ever catch a cold?
Even a virus has some pride.

What's the first thing a bass player says when he knocks on your door?
"Pizza delivery!"

A couple had been married for years and had not spoken a word to one another since soon after their wedding. They were eventually persuaded to seek counseling. The marriage counselor tried every technique he knew to stimulate communication between the couple, to no avail. Finally, he produced a large doublebass and began to play.

Soon after he began, the couple turned towards one another and began talking. Amazed, they stopped the counselor from playing and asked him how he had managed to break their silence. He answered "Well, EVERYBODY talks during a bass solo."

A man gives his son an electric bass for his 15th birthday, along with a coupon for four bass lessons. When the son returns from his first lesson, the father asks, "So, what did you learn?" "Well, I learned the first five notes on the E-string." Next week, after the second lesson, the father again asks about his progress, and the son replies, "This time I learned the first five notes on the A-string." One week later, the son comes home far later than expected, smelling of cigarettes and beer. So the father asks: "Hey, what happened in today's lesson?" "Dad, I'm sorry I couldn't make it to my lesson; I had a gig!"

A man goes to an exotic tropical island for a vacation. As the boat nears the island, he notices the constant sound of drumming coming from the island. As he gets off the boat, he asks the first native he sees how long the drumming will go on. The native casts about nervously and says, "Very bad when drumming stops."

At the end of the day, the drumming is still going and is starting to get on his nerves. So, he asks another native when the drumming will stop. The native looks as if he's just been reminded of something very unpleasant. "Very bad when drumming stops," he says, and hurries off.

After a couple of days with little sleep, our traveler is finally fed up, grabs the nearest native, slams him up against a tree, and shouts, "What the Hell happens when the drumming stops???" "Bass solo!"

A double bass player arrived a few minutes late for the first rehearsal of the local choral society's annual performance of Handel's Messiah. He picked up his instrument and bow, and turned his attention to the conductor. The conductor asked, "Would you like a moment to tune?" The bass player replied with some surprise, "Why? Isn't it the same as last year?"

At a rehearsal, the conductor stops and shouts to the bass section: "You are out of tune. Check it, please!"
The first bassist pulls all his strings, and says, "Our tuning is correct: all the strings are equally tight."
The first violist turns around and shouts, "You bloody idiot! It's not the tension. The pegs have to be parallel!"

Two bass players were engaged for a run of Carmen. After a couple of weeks, they each agreed to take an afternoon off in turn to go and watch the matinee performance from the front of the house.
Joe duly took his break; back in the pit that evening, Moe asked how it was.
"Great," says Joe. "You know that bit where the music goes `BOOM Boom Boom Boom' – well there are some guys up top singing a terrific song about a toreador at the same time."

There was a certain bartender who was quite famous for being able to accurately guess people's IQs. One night a man walked in and talked to him briefly and the bartender said, "Wow! You must have an IQ of about 140! You should meet this guy over here." So they talked for a while about nuclear physics and existential philosophy and had a great time.

A second man walked in and soon the bartender guessed an IQ of about 90 for him. So he sat him down in front of the big-screen TV and he watched football with the other guys and had a great of a time.

Then a third man stumbled in and talked to the bartender for a while. The bartender said to himself, "I think this guy's IQ must be about 29!" He took him over to a man sitting at a little table back in the corner and said, "You might enjoy talking with this guy for a while."

After the bartender left, the man at the table said, "So do you play French bow or German bow?"

Bowed
Instruments

String players' motto:
"It's better to be sharp than out of tune."

What's the difference between a viola and a cello?
A cello burns longer.

What's the difference between a cello and a coffin?
The coffin has the corpse on the inside.

Why did the cellist get mad at the timpanist?
He turned a tuning peg, and wouldn't tell which one.

How do you get a cellist to play fortissimo?
Write, "pp, espressivo."

How do you make a cello sound beautiful?
Sell it and buy a violin.

What's the difference between a fiddle and a violin?
No one minds if you spill beer on a fiddle.

Why do people tremble with fear when someone comes into a bank carrying a violin case?
They think he's carrying a machine gun and might be about to use it.
Why do people tremble with fear when someone comes into a bank carrying a violin case?
They think he's carrying a violin and might be about to use it.

Definition of a string quartet: a good violinist, a bad violinist, a would-be violinist and someone who hates the violin, getting together to complain about composers.

A string trio had been killed in a car accident, and they were standing before St. Peter in front of the Pearly Gates. The violinist stepped forward and addressed St. Peter, saying "Um...Hi, I guess I'm ready to go in."
St. Peter responded, "Okay. But first, you have to pass the test."

"What's the test?", asked the violinist.

"How do you spell God?", St. Peter asked.

"G-O-D," responded the violinist, and she walked on through to heaven.

Next, the cellist stepped forward and asked St. Peter, "How about me?"

Once again, St. Peter asked, "How do you spell God?"

"G-O-D," answered the cellist, and he passed through.

Finally, the violist stepped forward and confidently said, "Hey, St. Pete! G-O-D. That sure was easy." He began to step forward when his way was blocked by two seraphim. He turned to St. Peter and demanded, "What's the problem?"

St. Peter answered, "Don't be so hasty. How do you spell chrysanthemum?"

Why does a violinist have a handkerchief under his chin when he plays?

Because there's no spit valve.

Why are violas larger than violins?

They're not. The violist's head is smaller.

Glissando: Violinist's technique for difficult runs.

What do you do if you're short of a violinist?
Have a percussionist drag his fingernails across a chalk-board.

Why should you never drive a roof nail with a violin?
You might bend the nail.

Why are there so many violinists in an orchestra?
Because the conductor actually wants someone to play the right note.

Why do parents compliment their violist after a performance?
They heard the third violins.

What's the difference between a clarinet, a flute and a violin?

With the clarinet, the air comes out of the player's mouth and through the clarinet.

With the flute, the air comes out of the player's mouth and over the mouthpiece.

With the violin, the air goes in one ear and comes out the other.

How do you make a violin sound like a viola?
Sit at the back and don't play.

What are the requirements for the 2nd round of the International Viola Competition?
Holding the viola by memory.

Why can't you hear a viola on a digital recording?
Recording technology has reached such an advanced level of development that all extraneous noise is eliminated.

We all know that a viola is better than a violin because it burns longer. But why does it burn longer?
It's usually still in the case.

𝄞

What's the difference between a violist and a dog?
The dog knows when to stop scratching.

𝄞

In order to save money, the musicians decided to build their Union Hall themselves. As they proceeded to do the job, the hierarchy of the musicians was gradually reflected in the jobs that they did. The violists found themselves at the bottom of a ditch doing the nastiest of the digging. Above them, supervising, was a trumpet player. One violist turned to another and asked, "How come we're working down here and he's working up there?" The other responded, "I don't know, but I'll go up there and ask." The violist crawled up to the top of the ditch. "Why are we down there digging while you're up here supervising?" the violist asked the trumpeter. "Because I'm smarter than you," was the reply. "Huh, I don't understand," the confused violist said. "Allow me to demonstrate," said the trumpeter. He walked up to the nearest tree, put out his open hand in front of the tree and said to the violist, "Hit my hand!" The violist reared back with his fist and shot a punch at the trumpeter's open hand. At the last instant, the trumpeter moved his hand out of the way so that the violist's fist went slamming into the tree. "OW!," cried the violist, "I see what you mean." He then returned to the ditch and his friend waiting below. "Well," said the other violist, "did you find out why he's up there and we're down here?" "Yes," said the violist, whose hand was still throbbing, "it's because he's smarter than us." "I don't understand," said his friend. "Let me explain it to you," said the violist. He then took his open hand and placed it in front of his own face. "Now," he said, "hit my hand with your shovel!"

Two years ago an orchestra was on tour in France. One evening they decided to go find some snails so they could have escargots for dinner. Everybody was given a bag and sent into the vineyards.

Gradually, everybody came back with their bags filled with snails. All sections were there except the violists, who returned several hours later. The concertmaster asked, "Where have you been for so long and why are your bags empty?"

"Well," they said, "I don't know how you managed, but it was a disaster. We saw a lot of snails, but they were quick! Just as we went to get them, rush...and they were gone!"

What do a bad airplane mechanic and a violist have in common?
Both screw up Boeings.

Why are violists the only musicians without any problems in 7/8-time?
Because they count: one-two-three-four-five-six-se-ven-one-two....

What do violists and Mike Tyson have in common?
They both are hard on the ears.

Once there was a viola player who was second chair in the Winnipeg Symphony. He met a genie, who promised him three wishes. For his first wish, he asked to be a better musician, and he became first chair. For his second wish, he asked to be an even better musician, and he became first viola in the Berlin Symphony. For his third wish, he wished to be an even better musician, and he ended up playing second violin in the Winnipeg Symphony.

One day, the conductor of a no-name orchestra got seriously ill, so they pulled the second-to-last viola player to conduct for him. Everything went off without a hitch, and the orchestra sounded great! So, for the upcoming concert, they fired their old conductor and let the viola player do it. It was great! They got rave reviews, went on numerous tours all over the world, and became the most famous orchestra in history. Then, one day, the viola player told the concertmaster that he would like to go back and play, and could they hire a new conductor. So, the viola player went back to his seat, where his stand partner quickly asked, "Oh, and where have YOU been?"

After a major performance, this conductor throws a party. The next day the doorbell rings very early in the morning. The conductor's wife comes in and says, "Honey, there's a bunch of people in suits at the door." He says, "Don't worry, those are the violists. They are always late, and afraid to come in."

Johnny comes home from school, and says to his mom, "Mommy, I learned the alphabet today! The rest of the class messed up around F, but I made it all the way through!"

Johnny's mom says, "Very good, son. That's because you're a violist."

Johnny comes home the next day and screams, "Mommy, Mommy, I counted to a hundred today! Everyone else couldn't get past 60, but I made it all the way to 100!"

And his mom says, "Excellent. That's because you're a violist."

The next day, Johnny comes home and says, "Mommy, the teacher measured everyone's height in class today, and I was taller than everyone. Is that 'cause I'm a violist?"

His mom shakes her head and says, "No, honey; that's because you're twenty-six."

𝄞

A new viola player went into his first rehearsal with the orchestra, but when he sat down, all the other musicians were perplexed to see that he was wearing a set of headphones. The conductor asked him kindly: "Pardon me, but would you mind removing your headset, as we are about to begin?" The violist looked up, smiled dumbly, and said "I'd rather not." The conductor, not knowing what to do in such an odd situation, allowed the violist to keep his headphones on throughout the rehearsal. This same ritual continued on throughout the week, with the conductor asking the violist to remove the headphones, and the violist politely declining. Finally, the night of the concert arrived, and again, the violist arrived at the concert hall wearing the same set of headphones. Sure enough, the conductor spotted the violist still wearing his headphones. The conductor immediately took the violist aside backstage and demanded: "Look, I've let you wear these stupid things every minute of every rehearsal for a week now, but tonight is the concert. Now will you please TAKE THOSE DAMNED HEADPHONES OFF??!!!" As, usual the violist replied "I'd rather not." This was the straw that broke the camel's back. The conductor's face became as red as a beet, and he screamed at the top of his lungs "I SAID TAKE THOSE DAMN HEADPHONES OFF!!!!!" Reluctantly, the violist complied. The concert began smoothly, but about three minutes into the overture, the aforementioned violist dropped dead on stage. Amidst the confusion, the conductor found the violist's headphones and placed them on his head. What he heard was a simple CD looped message: "Breathe. . . Breathe. . . Breathe. . ."

What's the definition of a canon?
Two viola players trying to play the same part.

What is the difference between a violin and a viola?
About ten bucks.

How do you get a violist to play a downbow staccato?
Put a tenuto mark over a whole note and mark it solo.

A violist comes home late at night to discover fire trucks, police cars, and a smoking crater where his house used to be. The chief of police comes over to him and tells him, "While you were out, the conductor came to your house, killed your family, and burned it down." The violist replied, "You're kidding! The conductor came to my house?"

What do a viola and a lawsuit have in common?
Everyone is relieved when the case is closed.

Why are viola jokes so short?
So violinists can understand them.

How do you know if a viola section is at your front door?
Nobody knows when to come in.

If you throw a violist and a conductor off a tall building, who'll hit the ground first?
Who cares?

How do you know when a violin is out-of-tune?
When the bow's moving.

Why is a violin like a scud missile?
Both are offensive and inaccurate.

What's the difference between a violin and a fiddle?
A fiddle is fun to listen to.

Jacques Thibault, the violinist, was once handed an autograph book by a fan while in the greenroom after a concert. "There's not much room on this page," he said. "What shall I write?" Another violinist, standing by, offered the following helpful hint: "Write your repertoire."

"Haven't I seen your face before?" a judge demanded, looking down at the defendant.
"You have, Your Honor," the man answered hopefully, "I gave your son violin lessons last winter."
"Ah, yes," recalled the judge. "Twenty years!"

A female cellist stayed first chair because she kept her scherzo short.

How do you get a cello to play in tune?
Tell him the key signature has 8 sharps.

Once there was a violinist who got a gig to play a recital at a mental institution. He played the recital brilliantly and, backstage after the concert, he got a visit from one of the institutionalized patients.

"Oh, the concert you played was just lovely. The Paganini caprice was stunning, the counterpoint in the Bach came out so clearly, and the phrasing in your Debussy was just exquisite!", said the patient.

"Why, thank you," said the musician (thinking this person seemed pretty normal for an institutionalized person). "Are you by chance a musician?"

"Oh yes, I was concertmaster of an orchestra for many years, I've played all of the major concertos: Tchaikowsky, Brahms, Mozart, all the major ones." said the patient.

"Wow, that's impressive," said the violinist. "Did you do recitals as well?"

"Oh yes, I've done all the major sonatas, Bach, Kreisler, Vieuxtemps, all of the major ones," said the patient.

"Wow! Did you ever do chamber music?" asked the violinist.

"Oh yes. Duets, trios, quintets, sextets, all the major repertoire," said the patient.

Puzzled, the violinist asked "Did you ever play string quartets?"

All of a sudden, the patient went berserk and shouted "String quartets!... String quartets!... String quartets!... "

Drums

What do you call someone who hangs around with musicians?
A drummer.

What do you call soneone who hangs around with drummers?
Deaf.

A drummer's house is burning down. He runs next door to call the fire station. "Hurry, hurry. My house is burning to the ground!" "How do we get there?" the dispatcher asks. He sarcastically replies, "On your fire truck, DUH!"

What do you call a drummer with half a brain?
Gifted.

Be kind to animals - Feed the drummer before rehearsal!!

What did the drummer get on his IQ test?
Drool.

"Hey buddy, how late does the band play?"
"Oh, about a half a beat behind the drummer!"

How do you know you're dreaming?
The drummers are on the right beat!

How can you tell when a drummer is walking behind you?
You can hear his knuckles dragging on the ground.

Did you hear about the bass player who locked his keys in the car?
He had to break a window to get the drummer out!

Two cowboys were waiting in their fort for the Indians to attack. They listened to the distant pounding of war drums. One cowboy muttered to the other, "I don't like the sound of them drums."
Just then, a distant voice came over the hill, "It's not our usual drummer!"

What has three legs and an asshole on top?
A drum stool.

Why do bands have bass players?
To translate for the drummer.

Why are orchestra intermissions limited to 20 minutes?
So they don't have to retrain the drummers.

How do you know when a drummer is knocking at your door?
The knock always slows down.

How do you get a drummer to play an accelerando?
Ask him to play in 4/4 at a steady 120 bpm.

If thine enemy wrong thee, buy each of his children a drum.

I asked my drummer to spell "Mississippi"...
He said, "the river or the state?"

How do trumpet players manage to park in the handicap spots?
They put drumsticks on the dash.

How do you get a drummer to play his/her drums?
Start tuning your guitar.

How does a bass player get to a party?
He follows the drummer.

Did you hear about the drummer who could play a steady beat?
Me neither.

How many drummers does it take to drive from Boston to Memphis?
Two if you're in the Grateful Dead, one if you're in trouble because you've gotten your girlfriend pregnant and she's a groupie, and none if you're the drummer in the Jimi Hendrix Band.

How many drummers does it take to pop popcorn?
Two: One to hold the popper and one to shake the stove.

Support the arts, kill a drummer.

Have you heard of the drummer who finished college?
Me neither.

What are the two biggest lies told to drummers?
1. I'll meet you around the back and help you bring in your gear.
2. Don't worry...it's a simple Chick Corea tune in "9"; you'll pick it up...

𝄞

Why does the sound man say "1, 2, 1, 2" into the microphone?
So the drummer can make sure he has his sticks, 1, 2, 1, 2.

𝄞

Two drummers walk into a bar, which is actually kind of funny, because you would think that the second guy would have seen the first one do it.

𝄞

What do you call a dozen drummers at the bottom of the sea?
A good start!!

𝄞

One day a drummer sick of all of the "stupid drummer" jokes decided to change instruments. So he went to the local music store and said that he wanted to learn a new instrument. The store owner cheerfully replied OK and asked what he would be interested in playing. After looking around the shop he said I'll try those things over there, pointing to the accordion section.

After looking through the accordions for over an hour the store keeper said, "Have you found what you're looking for?"

The drummer replied, "Yes, I'll take that big red one over there."

The store keeper smiled and stared laughing. When the drummer asked why he was laughing the store keeper replied, "Are you a drummer, son?"

"Yeah!" replied the drummer.

"Well that big red thing is a radiator."

How many drummers does it take to wallpaper a room?
Three, if you slice them thin enough!

Why are drummers always losing their watches?
Everyone knows they have trouble keeping time.

What do you call a drummer who's lost his girlfriend?
Homeless.

𝄞

How do you call a drummer?
You can't. They don't pay their phone bills.

𝄞

What should you call a drummer?
It doesn't matter. They won't listen anyway.

𝄞

What's the best protection the Secret Service could have against a presidential assassination?
Make a drummer the Vice-President.

𝄞

A man was looking for a new brain. He went to a brain surgeon and told him of his problem. The surgeon said, "I only have three brains left." The man said, "Well which one's the cheapest?" The surgeon said, "I have a doctor's brain for cheap." The man said," We'll that's great, what else do you have?" The surgeon said, "I also have the brain of a rocket scientist, but that's just a little more pricey." The man replied, "Wow if you have the brain of a rocket scientist, the last one must be really smart." The surgeon said, "The most expensive one I have is a drummer's brain." The man said, "Why is a drummer's brain so expensive?" The surgeon replied, "We'll because it's never been used before."

𝄞

A lady walks into a store and tells the man behind the counter she would like some musicans' brains. "Alright" he says, "What kind?" "How much do they cost?" she asks. "Well, those there are trumpeters' at $ 5 a pound, those are French horns at $ 7 a pound, and those are conductors' at $ 10 a pound." He replies. "What are those way back there?" she asks. "Those are drummers' brains. They cost $ 100 a pound." He replies. "GOODNESS!!", she exclaims, "Why are they so expensive?" "Lady, do you realize how many drummers it takes to get a pound of brains?!?".

𝄞

What is the difference between a drummer and a savings bond?
One will mature and make money.

How can you get a drummer off your porch?
Pay for the pizza!

Why do drummers have lots of kids?
They're terrible at the rhythm method.

How can you make a drummer slow down?
Put a sheet of music in front of him.
How can you make that drummer stop?
Put notes on it!

How do you stop a drummer from playing?
Move the baton!

How do you get an elephant out of a 40-foot hole?
Lower a drummer into the hole and gross him out.

How many drummers can you fit in a phone booth?
None, "There's not enough room in there man!!"

An amateur drummer dies and goes to Heaven. While he is waiting outside the Pearly Gates, he hears some incredibly fast drumming coming from within Heaven. He immediately recognizes the playing, and asks St. Peter if that really is Buddy Rich playing drums in Heaven. St. Peter responds: "No, that's God. He just thinks that he's Buddy Rich."

What do you call a drummer driving a Volkswagon?
Farfromthinken.

Heard backstage: "Will the musicians and the drummer please come to the stage!"

To get this joke, you probably have to know about the legendary unpopularity of Buddy Rich amongst his band...

A horn player who had been playing with Buddy Rich for many years came back from vacation to hear a rumor that Buddy had died. He didn't quite believe it, so he phoned Buddy's wife and said, "Can I speak to Buddy please?"

Buddy's wife said, "I'm sorry, Buddy passed away last week."

"Oh, I'm sorry to hear that," he said, and hung up.

A couple of hours later, he called her again. "Is Buddy there please?"

"No, I'm sorry. Buddy's no longer with us," said Buddy's wife. And hung up the phone.

Ten minutes later, he called Buddy's wife again. "Can I speak to Buddy please?" he said.

She recognized his voice, and said: "Look, I've told you before, BUDDY'S DEAD!" And slammed down the phone.

Two minutes later, the phone rang again... "Is Buddy at home please?" the horn player asked.

Buddy's wife was furious. "I'm not going to tell you again, Buddy is dead. D. - E. - A. - D. DEAD! Why do you keep ringing me to ask for Buddy???!!!!"

He thought for a moment, and said: "I just love hearing you say it."

If a dollar bill was lying in the center of a room, and the Easter Bunny, Santa Claus, a drummer with good time, and a drummer with bad time were standing in the corners, who would get the money?

The drummer with bad time since the other three don't exist.

Two girls are walking along when they hear...

"Psst! Down here!"

They both look down and see a frog sitting beside the road. The frog says to them, "Hey, if you kiss me I'll turn into a world famous drummer and make you both rich and famous!" The two girls looked at each other, and one of them reached down and grabbed the frog and stuffed it in her pocket.

The other girl said, "What did you do that for?"

The first replied, "I'm not stupid. I know a talking frog is worth heaps more than a famous drummer any day!!!"

What is the difference between Santa Claus and a bass player?

Santa Claus has got gifts!

"Mom, when I grow up, I want to be a drummer."
His mother scoffs and replies...
"Well, you can't do both."

There's a bar with a bunch of drummers in it and they are all yelling "51 days, 51 days!" and more and more keep coming in, they are all ordering drinks and yelling "51 days! 51 days!" the bartender has a puzzled look on his face as more and more come into the bar, and order more and more drinks, and chant and chant. Finally, the bartender asks one of the drummers why they are all celebrating and chanting "51 days! 51 days!" The drummer answers with, "Well, we all just finished a puzzle in 51 days and the box said 2 to 4 years!"

What do you get if you cross a drummer with a gorilla?
A really dumb gorilla!!!

What's the last thing a drummer says in a band?
"Hey, guys - why don't we try one of my songs...?"

One day, a tuba player wanted to torture the drummer behind him, so he hid one of the drummer's sticks. After looking around for a few minutes, with a frantic, wide-eyed expression, the drummer fell to his knees, flung his arms wide, and screamed to Heaven: "Finally! A miracle. After all these years, I'm a conductor!"

♩

What did the professional drummer say when he got to his job?
"Would you like fries with that?"

♩

Why didn't the little drummer boy get into Heaven?
Because he woke the baby for Christ's sake!

♩

In New York City, an out-of-work jazz drummer named Ed was thinking of throwing himself off a bridge. But then he ran into a former booking agent who told him about the fantastic opportunities for drummers in Iraq. The agent said, "If you can find your way over there, just take my card and look up the bandleader named Faisal – he's the large guy with the beard wearing gold pajamas and shoes that curl up at the toes." Ed hit up everyone he knew and borrowed enough to buy transport to Iraq. It took several days to arrange for passport, visas, transportation into Iraq and the shipping of his equipment, but he was finally on his way.

Ed arrived in Baghdad and immediately started searching for Faisal. He found guys in pajamas of every color but gold. Finally, in a small coffeehouse, he saw a huge man with a beard – wearing gold pajamas and shoes that curled up at the toes! Ed approached him and asked if he was Faisal. He was. Ed gave him the agent's card and Faisal's face brightened into a huge smile.

"You're just in time – I need you for a gig tonight. Meet me at the market near the mosque at 7:30 with your equipment."

"But," gasped Ed, "what about a rehearsal?"

"No time – don't worry." And with that, Faisal disappeared.

Ed arrived in the market at 7:00 p.m. to set up his gear. He introduced himself to the other musicians, who were all playing instruments he had never seen in his life. At 7:30 sharp, Faisal appeared and hopped on the bandstand, his gold pajamas glittering in the twilight. Without a word to the musicians, he lifted his arm for the downbeat.

"Wait." shouted Ed. "What are we playing?"

Faisal shot him a look of frustration and shouted back, "Fake it! Just give me heavy afterbeats on 7 and 13."

Bodhran

What do you call a groupie who hangs around and annoys musicians?
A bodhran player.

What is the difference between a bodhran player and a terrorist?
Terrorists have sympathizers.

How do you know when there is a bodhran player at your front door?
The knocking gets faster and faster and faster.

What's the best thing to play a bodhran with?
A razor blade.

Brass

How do you make a trombone sound like a French horn?
Put your hand in the bell and miss a lot of notes.

How can you make a French horn sound like a trombone?
1. Take your hand out of the bell and lose all sense of taste.
2. Take your hand out of the bell and miss all of the notes!

Conductor: "Back to bar one."
French hornist, "My part doesn't have numbers."

How many French hornists does it take to play split lead?
One.

What is the difference between an old car without a muffler and a French horn?
The car without a muffler is more likely to be in tune.

What is the difference between a French horn section and a '57 Chevy?
You can tune a '57 Chevy.

How do you get your viola section to sound like the horn section?
Have them miss every other note.

How can you make a trombone sound like a French horn?
Stick your hand in the bell and play a lot of wrong notes.

How do horn players traditionally greet each other?
1. "Hi. I played that last year."
2. "Hi. I did that piece in junior high."

What do you get when you cross a French horn player with a goal post?
A goal post that can't march.

Why is the French horn a divine instrument?
Because man blows into it, but God only knows what comes out of it.

What's the difference between a dead snake in the road and a dead trombone player in the road?
1. The snake was going to a gig.
2. There are skid marks in front of the snake.

What is another term for trombone?
A wind-driven, manually operated pitch approximator!

What should you do if you run over a trombone?
Back up!

A man went into a novelty shop and saw an item that caught his fancy almost immediately. It was a stuffed rat. The man couldn't take his eyes off it, and finally asked how much it cost. The answer was "$ 79.95, but if you buy it, you can't return it for any reason." The man thought this was a bit odd, but he was really taken by the stuffed rat so he bought it.
As he headed down the street with the stuffed rat, several live rats started following him. He thought this was really odd, but he kept walking. Within a few blocks, he had a huge pack of rats behind him. When he got to the river, he

threw the stuffed rat into the river, and all the live rats jumped into the river and drowned. The man returned to the shop. As soon as he walked in, the owner said "I told you you couldn't return the stuffed rat!"
The man said, "No! I don't want to return it! I was wondering if you had any stuffed trombone players."

A trombonist just died and is on his way to Heaven. He is feeling great, for he thinks he never has to play that instrument again. When he visits the Holy Announcement Board, he sees that the rehearsal of the Holy Orchestra is to be at 4 p.m. on clouds 30-40. So he goes there and sees a giant orchestra, consisting of 1 million violins, 800,000 violas, 600,000 cellos, 400,000 basses, 50,000 each woods, 40,000 trumpets and 10,000 timpani, but he just cannot find any trombones. Then, after a while, he sees one lonely trombonist who is really happy to get company. The piece starts and about a million violins start playing a soft ppp, then about 800,000 violas come in, then the 600,000 cellos, then 400,000 basses, then 50,000 clarinets, 50,000 oboes and bassoons, 40,000 trumpets and everything is still at p. Then comes the first cue for the 10,000 timpani and now, finally, there is the first cue for the 2 trombones. They play their first note and the conductor breaks up, screaming, "Trombones, too loud!"

What's the difference between a talented hockey player and a talented trombone player?
Hockey players are supposed to hurt people with their talents.

What's the formula for the number of McDonald's employees in a trombone section?
Total number of players minus the number of Burger King employees, minus the number unemployed.

What did the trombone player do when he won the lottery?
Silly, you know trombone players can't afford tickets!

Trombonists never die, they just slide away.

In an orchestral arrangement, what's the difference between the third trombone part and the tuba part?
The bassoon cues.

What is a trombone?
A slide whistle with delusions of grandeur!

What's the difference between a trombone and a sewer?
Less water flows through the sewer, and it's cleaner too.

What do you say when you meet a bass trombone player who can improvise?
1.   "Need... Wa... Wah... Water...(thud)"
2.   "They're coming to take me away, ha ha!"
3.   "Maybe that was one too many beers."
4.   "How long will your tenor be in the shop?"
5.   "I must be dead, but is this Heaven or Hell?"

How can you tell when a bass trombone is out of tune?
The bass trombonist is also present.

What's the difference between a valve trombone and a baritone horn?
If you run over a baritone nobody cares. If you run over a valve trombone, every real trombonist in the world thanks you.

It is difficult to trust anyone whose instrument changes shape as he plays it!

What's the difference between a bass trombone and a chain saw?
1. Vibrato, though you can minimize the difference by holding the chain saw very still.
2. It's easier to improvise on a chain saw.

How do you know when a trombone player is at your door?
The doorbell drags.

What do you call a trombonist with a beeper and a cell phone?
An optimist.

How do you improve the aerodynamics of a trombonist's car?
Take the Domino's Pizza sign off the roof.

What is the difference between a dead trombone player lying in the road, and a dead squirrel lying in the road?
The squirrel might have been on his way to a gig.

What kind of calendar does a trombonist use for his gigs?
"Year-At-A-Glance."

What is the dynamic range of a bass trombone?
On or off.

How can you tell which kid on the playground is the child of the trombonist?
He/She can't swing and doesn't know how to use the slide.

Conductor: "Guys, I need you to play with more dynamics!"
One of the trumpet players: "But boss, that's already as loud as we can play!"

Why did the trumpet player play a loud, blaring jazz solo during a slow, soft symphonic movement?
Because the part was marked tacit, and he thought it said "Take it!"

In an emergency, a female jazz trumpeter was hired to do some solos with a symphony orchestra. Everything went fine through the first movement, when she had some really hair-raising solos, but in the second movement she started improvising madly when she wasn't supposed to play at all. After the concert the conductor came round looking for an explanation. She said, "I looked in the score and it said 'tacit' – so I took it!"

What's the best recording of the Haydn Trumpet Concerto?
Music Minus One.

How are trumpets like pirates?
They are both murder on the high C's.

Three famous trumpet players are up in an airplane. One of them says, "I'll throw out a 100 dollar bill and make someone very happy." The one next to him says, "I'll throw out two 50 dollar bills, and make two people very happy." The other one said, "I'll throw five 20's out the door, and make five people happy." The pilot, who was their conductor, said, "Why don't you all three jump, and make the whole band very happy?"
(How did the trumpet players get that much money in the first place?)

𝄞

Before a rehearsal, you can usually see the clarinet, saxophone, and double reed players quietly sucking on reeds. Too bad trumpet players aren't shut up that easily.

𝄞

If you are a stone's throw away from a trumpeter, what should you do?
Throw stones.

𝄞

What do you call a person playing a trumpet in public?
Suicidal.

What do you call a beautiful woman on a trumpet player's arm?
A tattoo.

How do you know when a trumpet player is at your door?
The doorbell shrieks!

Why can't a gorilla play trumpet?
He's too sensitive.

What is the pre-programmed message on a lead trumpet player's Emergency MedAlert Button?
"HELP! I'M PLAYING...AND I CAN'T CUT OFF!"

What do you call two trumpet players and three tuba players walking into a strip club?
Horny.

𝄞

What's the range of a tuba?
Twenty yards, if you've got a good arm.

𝄞

What's the difference between a tuba player and a dead guy who was once strung out on drugs and wore gay clothing and had no purpose in life because he lived with his parents and he had no money? The dead guy is dead.

𝄞

Tuba player: Did you hear my last recital?
Friend: I hope so.

𝄞

Why would a tuba player get fired from any office job?
He's a low character, below the staff, and he spends too much time resting.

𝄞

"Did you hear about the tuba player on the walk from the law?"

"Don't you mean 'on the run'?"

"Come on, when was the last time you saw a tuba player running?"

Why should you have to be a tuba player to work for a furnace repair service?

Tuba players know everything about hot air!

What's half of a tuba?

A one-ba!

There are two tuba players sitting in a car. Who's driving?

The policeman.

What do you clean your sousaphone with?

With a tuba toothpaste.

Woodwinds

Small wonder we have so much trouble with air pollution in the world when so much of it has passed through saxophones.

How do you put down a saxophone?
Call it a bassoon.

What's a bassoon good for?
Kindling for an accordion fire.

How many bassoonists does it take to eat a possum?
Two. One to eat, one to watch for traffic.

What is better? A bassoon or an oboe?
A bassoon – it makes more tooth picks.

Why is a bassoon better than an oboe?
The bassoon burns longer.

What is a burning oboe good for?
Setting a bassoon on fire.

How do you make an oboe player quit his job?
Give him 50 cents!

What's the difference between an oboe and an onion?
Nobody cries when you chop up an oboe.

Did you hear about the successful hunter's secret to attracting so many ducks?
He paid an oboe player to go along with him and play.

Top Ten Reasons To Play The Oboe

10. People pay attention long enough to figure out what the heck that thing is that you're playing.
9. Learning to transpose music as you play (from reading flute parts).
8. The case is a good weapon in emergencies; bigger than a flute case, can act as a shield and yet is still portable!
7. If you lose your music, the bells always have the same part.
6. If you lose your music, the flutes always have the same part.
5. If you lose your music, somebody at some point in the piece has the same part!!
4. You can always hide in the clarinet section.
3. No one cares if you're not heard.
2. You always get your own stand.
1. No competition!! (At least, not in the same band)

What's the difference between an oboist and a psychiatric ward patient?
The oboist just hasn't been caught yet.

Five Reasons Not To Play the Oboe

5. Oboe reeds are more expensive than clarinet and sax reeds.
4. Having to learn to transpose music as you play (because there's not an oboe part in at least half the pieces the band will perform!)
3. Having to explain that it's an oboe and not a clarinet, every single day. (It will also be incumbent upon you to explain what the water is for. Only every other day, but it takes longer to explain why you have to soak your reed in water instead of using spit, especially for regular reed instrument players.)
2. Flutes hitting you in the shoulder.
1. Cutting your tongue on the reed.

A conductor calls the doctor to find out what to do after the oboist swallows her reed. The doctor replies, "Have you tried muted trumpet?"

What's the difference between an oboe playing in tune and Star Trek?
Star Trek could actually happen one day.

What's the definition of a "half step?"
Two oboes playing in unison.

What's the definition of a "major second?"
Two baroque oboes playing in unison.

How do you get an oboist to play A flat?
Take the batteries out of his electronic tuner.

What's the difference between a scud missile and a bad oboist?
A bad oboist can kill you.

How do you get a clarinetist out of a tree?
Cut the noose.

Why don't they make mutes for clarinets?
It would be a waste of time – it would take a lot more than
a mute to make a clarinet sound good!

What is the best use for duct tape?
Taping a clarinetist's mouth closed.

What's the definition of a nerd?
Someone who owns his own clarinet.

How do you prevent an oboe from being stolen?
Put it in a clarinet case.

In hospital, what's the difference between the use of a clarinet and a saxophone?
The saxophone is used to lull crying babies to sleep, and the clarinet to wake coma patients.

Why aren't there very many alto clarinet jokes?
Most people have better things to do with their time.

How do you put down a tenor saxophone?
Confuse it with a bass clarinet.

What's the purpose of the bell on a bass clarinet?
Storing the ashes from the rest of the instrument.

You hardly ever see a flutist take a breath because they have a vast supply of air in their heads.

On the other hand...
Why are there so few flute jokes?
None of the other instrumentalists are smart enough to think of any.

What is the definition of perfect pitch in a piccolo?
When you throw it in the toilet and it doesn't hit the rim.

What's the difference between a piccolo and a dog whistle?
1. The what between a piccolo and a dog whistle?
2. Dog whistles are played by men to attract dogs.
3. If you have good ears, you can hear a dog whistle.
4. A dog whistle irritates only one species.
5. Tuning.
6. In a marching band, the dog whistle is dangerous, whereas the piccolo is merely useless.
7. The price.
8. The value.
9. People with dog whistles usually know how to play them.
10. You can't tune a piccolo.

Two guys are out driving through a neighborhood. The guy who's driving notices that the neighborhood dogs have started barking their heads off. "Hey, why are all the dogs barking together?" he asks his friend. His friend leans back in his seat and answers, "Oh, the flutes are tuning at the high school across the street." They drive on to another neighborhood, about 10 miles from the other high school. There, the dogs are running around like maniacs and whining like crazy. The guy who's driving asks, "What's going on with the dogs in THIS neighborhood?" His friend answers, "Don't you know? The high school back there has 4 piccolos."

What key is the alto flute pitched in?
G – I really don't care, either!!

Two musicians are walking down the street, and one says to the other, "Who was that piccolo I saw you with last night?"
The other replies, "That was no piccolo, that was my fife."

How can you tell if a 747 loaded with flute players has just landed?
The jet engines stop, but the whining continues!

One day, a saxophone player was driving down the freeway when he hit two flute players who were crossing the road. One went through the windshield and the other flew about thirty feet down the road. When the policeman interviewed him, he said, "Oh, you're a sax player too, huh? Well I think I know how we can get these two flutists. I can arrest one for breaking and entering, and the other for leaving the scene of the crime."

What's the difference between a saxophone and a lawn mower?
1. Lawn mowers sound better in small ensembles.
2. The neighbors are upset if you borrow a lawnmower and don't return it.
3. The grip.

What's the definition of a minor second?
Two flutists playing in unison.

What's the difference between a lawn mower and a soprano sax?
You can tune a lawn mower.

What do a saxophone and a baseball have in common?
People cheer when you hit them with a bat.

You may be a redneck saxophonist if ...
... you have an old bass sax up on blocks in your front yard.
... you spell it "saxaphone".
... you think the bell of your instrument is a great place to hold an ice-cold longneck during a gig.
... the gun rack in your pickup truck holds a couple of old Buesher sopranos.

A saxophone player dies, and, as Heaven seems quite boring to him, he finally gets permission to visit Hell for an hour. As he opens the door to the music hall down there, he sees the Devil conducting an All Star big band with a free chair right between Parker and Coltrane. Immediately he goes back and tells God: "This is it, I'm going to switch for good!" A little later he sits playing next to his idols, but the whole band seems to vamp on the last shout chorus for hours. Eventually he gets up and asks the Devil: "Excuse me Sir, when are we going to play the coda?" In response, the Devil just grins...

As a guy walks through a forest, a fairy suddenly appears and offers him a free wish, whatever it might be. So he takes out a pocket atlas and points towards different continents: "See, here is suffering, there is hunger, and over there people are tortured. I want all people to be free and healthy! Can you do that?" The fairy sighs and says: "Well, this is very hard, even for me. Is there a chance that you can come up with another wish instead that would make it a little easier?" The guy answers: "As a matter of fact, there is. See, I play the soprano saxophone, and I have such a hard time with the intonation in the upper register. Do you think you could..." "Okay, okay, let's look at your atlas one more time..."

Why did the lead alto player play so many wrong notes?
Because he kept ignoring the key signature – he thought it
was a suggestion.

Why can't alto saxophonists stay married?
Blaming it on the reed doesn't work.

What's the difference between the creationist theory of the
origin of life and a tenor sax?
The theory doesn't have as many leaks.

Two bari sax players were in the Small Offences Court. The
magistrate asks one of them, "Why are you here?" He
answers, "For throwing flowers in the lake, M'Lord." The
magistrate then asks the other one, "Why are you here?"
And the other bari man says, "I'm Flowers!"

How many C melody sax players can you fit into a phone booth?
Both of them.

How many psychologists does it take to change a sax mouthpiece?
Only one, but the mouthpiece must be willing to change!

Why did the chicken cross the road?
To get away from the bassoon recital.

What do you call a sax player who only plays endless phrases of 64th notes at a furious tempo?
A ballad specialist!

What's the difference between a bari sax and a chain saw?
The exhaust.

If you were lost in the woods, who would you trust for directions: an in-tune sax player, an out-of-tune sax player, or Santa Claus?
The out-of-tune sax player. The other two indicate you've been hallucinating.

How does a sax player handle a difficult part of the score?
He starts to change his reed!

Vocals

How do you know there's a female vocalist at your door?
She's knocking because she can't find her key!

What's the difference between a soprano and the PLO?
You can negotiate with the PLO.

What's the difference between a soprano and a drink machine?
With the drink machine, you might actually get a Hi-C.

What is the difference between a soprano and a pit bull?
The jewelry, darling, the jewelry!

What's the definition of an alto?
A soprano who can sight-read.

How do you make a soprano shut up?
Stop her tape recording.

How can you tell if a Wagnerian soprano is dead?
The horses all seem relieved.

If you threw a violist and a soprano off a cliff, which one would hit the ground first?
1. The violist. The soprano would have to stop halfway down to ask directions.
2. Who cares?

What is the difference between a soubrette and a cobra?
One is deadly poisonous, and the other is a reptile.

A jazz musician dies and goes to Heaven. He is told "Hey man, welcome! You have been elected to the Jazz All-Stars of Heaven – right up there with Satchmo, Miles, Django, all the greats. We have a gig tonight. Only one problem – God's girlfriend gets to sing."

Why are most soprano jokes all one-liners?
So tenors can understand them.

What do a woman in labor and a tenor have in common?
They both strain.

How do you tell if a tenor is dead?
The wine bottle is still full and the comics haven't been touched.

What do you see if you look up a soprano's skirt?
A tenor.

How do you put a sparkle in a soprano's eye?
Shine a flashlight in her ear.

Where is a tenor's resonance?
Where his brain should be.

What's the definition of a male quartet?
Three men and a tenor.

Did you hear about the tenor who announced that in the following season he would only sing three title roles?
Othello, Samson, and Forza del Destino. (true story)

If you took all the tenors in the world and laid them end to end, it would be a good idea.

How do you tell if a bass is actually dead?
Hold out a check (but don't be fooled: a slight, residual spasmodic clutching action may occur even hours after death).

In the last act of Don Giovanni, there is always a statue which is replaced at some point by a real singer, a bass (the Commendatore). How can you tell when the switch has occurred?

The "statue" starts looking a bit stiff.

What is the difference between the men's final at Wimbledon and a high school choral performance?

The tennis final has more men.

How does a young man become a member of a high school chorus?

On the first day of school he turns into the wrong classroom.

What is the difference between a world war and a high school choral performance?

The performance causes more suffering.

Why do high school choruses travel so often?
Keeps assassins guessing.

What's the definition of an optimist?
A choral director with a mortgage.

What is the difference between a high school choral director and a chimpanzee?
It's scientifically proven that chimpanzees are able to communicate with humans.

What do you call a girl that hangs around with musicians?
A singer.

If the singer and drummer got into a fight, who would win? It's a trick question. There would be no fight. The singer would whine until he got his way!

One night, a lounge piano player pulls over the singer and says, "Now tonight we'll try a special version of this song: after five and a half measures of intro you come in with the second verse a minor third up, go to the bridge after 11 bars, twice modulate a half step down, and halfway in the last A-section you start the tag, but a tritone lower. Are you ready? One, two,..." "Hell, wait!" the singer interrupts. "I'll never be able to do this!" The pianist replies, "But you nailed it last night!"

Heckler: Can you sing tenor?
Singer: Of course.
Heckler: TEN OR twelve miles away!

Conductor

What do you do with a bad conductor?
Stand next to him during a thunderstorm.

What does "Accelerando" mean?
Hurry up, the conductor skipped another page again.

Why are conductors' hearts so coveted for transplants?
They've had so little use.

What does a good conductor weigh?
28 ounces, not counting the urn.

If you throw a conductor and a violist off a tall building, who'll hit the ground first?
Who cares?

What's the difference between a bull and a symphony orchestra?
The bull has its horns in front and its ass in the back.

What's black and brown and looks good on a conductor?
A Doberman.

What's the difference between a railroad conductor and an orchestral conductor?
Well, one controls the train, while the other...

What's the difference between an orchestra and a freight train?
A freight train needs a conductor!

Why did they bury the conductor 20 feet into the earth?
Because deep down he was a nice guy.

The definition of a conductor:
Someone who is able to follow many people at once.

A man and a boy were taking a walk through the cemetery. The boy said, "Look, Daddy, here's a grave where two people are buried!" The father said, "Two people? Let me look." So the father took a look, and sure enough, the marker said, "Here lies a symphony conductor and a humble man."

Top Ten things You Will Never Hear Said By A Music Director...

10. Okay saxophones, play that even louder now!
9. Wow drummers, you got that right the first time!
8. Can we have the whole soprano section sing the high note?
7. Your tuning is great today basses!
6. Let's just have fun today!
5. It's OK to talk during solos, drummers!
4. Let's include a drum set on that!
3. You can get drunk before the concert basses, I'm going to!
2. That was real good, violas!
1. I'm sorry, it's all my fault!

Quotes attributed to Eugene Ormandy:

* "Who is sitting in that empty chair?"
* "If you don't have it in your part, leave it out because there is enough missing already."
* "I need one more bass less."
* "We can't hear the balance yet, because the soloist is on the plane."
* "Thank you for your co-operation and vice versa."
* "I never say what I mean, but I always manage to say something similar."
* "I don't want to confuse you more than absolutely necessary."

We took a collection for our band director's funeral asking $ 50 from community leaders. We got $ 100 with a note to bury two of them.

What has 32 feet, and an IQ of 33?
The flag core.

Top ten ways to upset your drum major

10. Listen intently to his instructions. Do exactly the opposite. Insist that that was what he said to begin with.

9. Empty spit exactly in the spot where he steps down from the podium. Get the entire brass section to do this. Often.

8. Harass the cheerleaders. Blame the comments on the drum major.

7. Invent your own tempo. Stick to your guns, no matter how big his beats are or how much he glares at you.

6. "Confess" to your band director that you just can't follow such bad conducting and obscured beats.

5. Drop vital instrument parts during drill (this includes bells, foot joints, slides, etc...

4. Wait until he's just finished an hour of basics reviewing. "Forget" to step off on your left foot. Repeatedly.

3. Whenever you see him trying to find his tempo, immediately start singing, playing, or tapping your foot loudly and out of tempo. Annoyingly infectious songs or songs in a completely different meter are especially effective.

2. Wait until the busses have left before looking surprised and announcing loudly, "No one told us to take our uniforms off the bus, too!" or "You mean they aren't coming back to unload the instruments?!" NOTE: the above are best performed by at least three people for maximum chaos.

And the number one way to upset your drum major is:

1. In your sweetest and most respectful voice, ask him, "As God, why can't you make our team win a game?" Look serious. Expect an answer. Wait for one.

Additional suggestions:

Leave an important uniform or instrument pieces in the stands. Leave another one when you go to get it. Works best if you use a stupified look when asked where said object is.

Top Ten Ways To Know You've Been In A Band Too Long:

10. You actually like marching and would kill to do it year round.
9. The drummers start to make sense to you.
8. You stay in step with the people around you when you walk.
7. You conduct to the songs on the radio.
6. You wonder what life will be like after the band.
5. You roll step while walking to class.
4. You think "Louie, Louie" is the best song ever written.
3. You major in music in college and use your band director as a role model.

2. You start screaming "LEFT", "LEFT", "LEFT" to the people that walk in front of you on the way to class.

1. You can relate to three or more of the above.

𝄞

What do drum line members do after they graduate from high school?
Retire and live off social security.

𝄞

Why is a conductor like a condom?
It's safer with one, but more fun without.

𝄞

What's the difference between God and a conductor?
God knows He's not a conductor.

𝄞

What's the definition of an assistant conductor?
A mouse trying to become a rat.

𝄞

What's the difference between alto clef and Greek?
Some conductors actually read Greek.

It was the night of the big symphony concert, and all the town notables showed up to hear it. However, it was getting close to 8 o'clock and the conductor hadn't yet shown up. The theater's manager was getting desperate, knowing that he'd have to refund everyone's money if he cancelled the concert, so he went backstage and asked all the musicians if any of them could conduct.

None of them could, so he went around and asked the staff if any of them could conduct. He had no luck there either, so he started asking people in the lobby, in the hope that maybe one of them could conduct the night's concert.

He still hadn't found anyone, so he went outside and started asking everybody passing by if they could conduct. He had no luck whatsoever, and by this time the concert was 15 minutes late in starting. The assistant manager came out to say that the crowd was getting restless and about ready to demand their money back.

The desperate manager looked around and spied a cat, a dog, and a horse standing in the street. "Oh, what the heck," he exclaimed. "Let's ask them – what do we have to lose?"

So the manager and assistant manager went up to the cat, and the manager asked: "Mr. cat, do you know how to conduct?" The cat meowed: "I don't know, I'll try," but though it tried really hard, it just couldn't stand upright on its hind legs. The manager sighed and thanked the cat, and then moved on to the dog.

"Mr. dog," he asked, "do you think you can conduct?" The dog woofed: "Let me see," but although it was able to stand up on its hind legs and wave its front paws around, it just couldn't keep upright long enough to last through an entire movement.

"Well, nice try," the manager told the dog, and with a sigh of resignation turned to the horse. "Mr. horse," he asked, "how about you – can you conduct?" The horse looked at him for a second and then without a word turned around, presented its hind end, and started swishing its tail in perfect four-four time.

"That's it!" the manager exclaimed, "the concert can go on!" However, right then the horse dropped a load of plop onto the street. The assistant manager was horrified, and he told the manager: "We can't have this horse conduct! What would the orchestra think?"

The manager looked first at the horse's rear end and then at the plop lying in the street and replied, "Trust me – from this angle, the orchestra won't even know they have a new conductor!"

Once upon a time, there was a blind rabbit and blind snake, both living in the same neighborhood. One beautiful day, the blind rabbit was hopping happily down the path toward his home, when he bumped into someone. Apologizing profusely he explained: "I'm blind, and didn't see you there."

"Perfectly all right," said the snake, "because I'm blind, too, and didn't see to step out of your way."

A conversation followed, gradually becoming more intimate, and finally the snake said: "This is the best conversation I have had with anyone for a long time. Would you mind if I felt you to see what you are like?"

"Why, no," said the rabbit. "Go right ahead."

So the snake wrapped himself around the rabbit and shuffled and snuggled his coils, and said: "MMMM! You're soft and warm and fuzzy and cuddly...and those ears! You must be a rabbit."

"Why, that's right!" said the rabbit. "May I feel you?"

"Go right ahead." said the snake, stretching himself out full length on the path.

The rabbit began to stroke the snake's body with his paws, then drew back in disgust. "Yuck!" he said. "You're cold...and slimy... you must be a conductor!"

A guy walks into a pet store wanting a parrot. The store clerk shows him two beautiful ones out on the floor. "This one's $ 5,000 and the other is $ 10,000." the clerk said. "Wow! What does the $ 5,000 one do?"

"This parrot can sing every aria Mozart ever wrote."

"And the other?" said the customer.

"This one can sing Wagner's entire Ring cycle. There's another one in the back room for $ 30,000."

"Holy moly! What does that one do?"

"Nothing that I can tell, but the other two parrots call him 'Maestro'."

A violinist was auditioning for an orchestra in England. After his audition he was talking with the conductor. "What do you think about Brahms?" asked the conductor.

"Ah..." the violinist replied, "Brahms is a great guy! Real talented musician. In fact, he and I were just playing some duets together last week!"

The conductor was impressed. "And what do you think of Mozart?" he asked him.

"Oh, he's just swell! I just had dinner with him last week!" replied the violinist. Then the violinist looked at his watch and said he had to leave to catch the 1:30 train to London.

Afterwards, the conductor was discussing him with the board members. He said he felt very uneasy about hiring this violinist, because there seemed to be a serious credibility gap. The conductor knew for certain that there was no 1:30 train to London.

A new conductor was at his first rehearsal. It was not going well. He was as wary of the musicians as they were of him. As he left the rehearsal room, the timpanist sounded a rude little "bong." The angry conductor turned and said, "All right! Who did that?"

Bagpipes

Why do bagpipers walk when they play?
To get away from their own noise.

Did you know the Irish invented the bagpipes as a joke?
The Scots haven't gotten it yet.

What's the difference between a bagpiper and a terrorist?
Terrorists have sympathizers.

Angus was asked why there were drones on the bagpipe when they make such a distressing sound. He answered, "Without the drones, I might as well be playing the piano."

What would you do if you had all the bagpipe players on earth lined up end-to-end, to the moon and back?
Leave them there.

What does one bagpipe player never say to another?
"Hey man, what key's it in?"

I thought learning to play the bagpipes was hard, until I realized I was just strangling an ostrich!

How can you tell if a bagpipe is out of tune?
Someone is blowing into it.

The young Scotsman left his home in Scotland to study at an English university. After a month, his mother came to visit him in the residence hall where he was living with other students.

"How do you find the English students, Donald?" she asked.

"Mother," he replied, "they're such noisy people! The one in the room on that side keeps banging his head on the wall all night, and the one in the room on this side screams all night long."

"Donald, how do you manage to put up with such noisy neighbors?"

"I ignore them. I just mind my own business and keep playing my bagpipes."

Where do you put a capo on a set of bagpipes?
Around the piper's neck.

Keyboards

There were two men sitting next to each other in a pub having a few beers together. One of the men turns to the other and says, "Psst, do you wanna see what I've got in my pocket?". And the other man says, "OK, what?" To the amazement of this man, the other man takes out of his pocket a little man playing a piano. "My goodness! Where did you get that?", asks the guy. "Shhh, it's a secret. You see I've got this magic stone, all you have to do is rub it three times and wish for whatever you want." The man eagerly agreed, and took the stone in his hand and rubbed it three times. Closing his eyes he said, "I wish to be covered in money." And in an instant, the man found himself smothered in gallons of sticky honey. "Hey! I said 'money', NOT 'honey'!", cried the man. "Ah! Did you honestly think I wanted a 12-inch pianist?"

What do you get if you throw a piano down a mine shaft?
A flat miner.

What do you get if you drop a piano on an army base?
A flat major.

Why was the piano invented?
So the musician would have a place to put his beer.

The audience at a piano recital was appalled when a telephone rang just off stage. Without missing a note, the soloist glanced toward the wings and called, "If that's my agent, tell him I'm working!"

How can you tell if your keyboard player is getting better? He'll tell you!

How can you tell if a keyboard player is knocking at your door?
He rings the doorbell instead!

How can you tell if there is a synth player at your door?
You think you hear him knocking, but you're not quite sure.

The organ is the instrument of worship, for in its sounding we sense the Majesty of God, and in its ending we know the Grace of God.

Accordion

What's the difference between an accordion and a lawn mower?
If you put both on Home Shopping Network, you could sell the lawn mower.

Who's the patron saint of accordionists?
Our Lady of Spain.

An accordion is just a bagpipe with pleats.

An accordionist and a banjo player are hired to play on New Year's Eve.
At the end of the party, the guy who hired them says, "You guys were great. You want to play for me again next New Year's Eve?"
The accordion player says, "Sure. Do you mind if we leave our gear?"

To be a good bandoneon player, you have to be schizophrenic and both of you have to be excellent typists.

What's an accordion good for?
Learning how to fold maps.

What do you call an accordion player with a beeper?
An optimist.

Why doesn't Heaven have a pipe organ?
Because they needed the keys in Hell to make accordions.

Terrorists have taken 90 accordion players hostage, and if their demands aren't met, they'll release one every hour.

Minimum safe distances between street musicians and the public:
Violinist: 25 feet
Bad violinist: 50 feet
Tone deaf guitar player who knows 3 chords: 75 feet
15-year-old electric guitar player with Nirvana fixation: 100 feet
Accordionist: 60 miles

An accordion player in his middle 40's was driving home around 10:00 p.m. from a Bar Mitzva. When he left, he placed his instrument in the back window of his car so he could watch it while he drove to make sure it was OK. On his way, he decided to stop at a bar and get a drink to make up for the boring night. He stopped, locked his car, and then went inside. After he had had about 3 drinks, he suddenly realized where he had put the accordion! He should have remembered what happened last time he left it in his back window! So he ran outside and looked at his car. The back window was broken in, and glass was all over the place. And, sure enough, there were two more accordions!!!

When you arrive in Heaven, St. Peter says, "Welcome to Heaven! Here's your harp."
When you arrive in Hell, Satan says, "Welcome to Hell! Here's your accordion."

What is worse than a bad accordion player?
A good accordion player.

Banjo

What's the difference between a banjo and a chain saw?
The chain saw has a greater dynamic range.

What's the least used sentence in the English language?
"Is that the banjo player's Porsche?"

What's the second-least used sentence in the English Language?
"I respect that banjo player for his mind."

What's the definition of "perfect pitch"?
When you toss the banjo in the dumpster and it lands on the accordion.

Why do banjo players prefer picking instead of strumming?
Because an acquired skill is more easily transferred than learning a new skill.

What's the fastest way to tune a banjo?
With wire cutters.

Why do so many fishermen own banjos?
1. They make great anchors.
2. They make great paddles.

Frets ain't nothing but speed bumps on a banjo.

Listener: Can you read music?
Banjo player: not enough to hurt my playing.

A guy walks into a bar and announces, "Hey, I got a great new banjo joke!" The bartender says, "Let me stop you right there, son. You see that karate black belt hangin' up behind the bar? That's mine. And I play the banjo. See that mean lookin' feller in the Harley T-shirt. That's my brother - and HE plays the banjo. And that big ugly old guy in the corner with the big scar across his face? That's my Pa - and he plays the banjo. NOW, are you sure you wanna tell that banjo joke in here?" "Well, no. Not if I'm gonna hafta EXPLAIN it three times!"

What's the difference between a banjo player and a frog?
A frog might get a gig.

How does the discerning banjo listener tell one banjo song from another?
Different names.

What do you say to a banjo player in a three-piece suit?
"Will the defendant please rise?"

There's nothing I like better than the sound of a banjo, unless of course it's the sound of a chicken caught in a vacuum cleaner.

What's the best way to play a banjo?
With a hacksaw.

Harp

What's the definition of a quarter tone?
A harpist tuning unison strings.

Harp players spend half their time tuning their instrument and the other half playing out of tune.

Why are harps like elderly parents?
Both are unforgiving and hard to get into and out of cars.

How long does a harp stay in tune?
About 20 minutes...or until someone opens a door.

June, the harpist, and Sam, the trombonist, went out to a discotheque. Sam's car wouldn't lock, but Sam knew the owner so they locked their instruments in his office. Having too much to drink, they went back to rehearsal without their instruments. June told the conductor, "I left my harp in Sam's friend's disco."

Chang

(A "Chang" is a Central Asian instrument used in countries such as Uzbekistan. It's something like a hammered dulcimer with a damper pedal.)

How long does it take to tune a chang?
Nobody knows.

Why is it so difficult to tune a chang?
So that a violist can feel superior about something.

How many chang players does it take to change a light-bulb?
All of them. One to twist the bulb for several hours, and the other one to decide that it's as good as it's going to get, and that they might as well flip the switch.

The return of the lightbulb

This is a special section of the book, but nevertheless inevitable. We've already learned a lot about this mysterious species commonly known as a musician. But to fully understand his complex, hitherto unexplored, brain (or whatever his skull may contain) we need scientific assistance. Leading authorities of anthropology have developed a highly evolved test program to at least try to understand the behavior of this form of life which mostly walks upright. The test appears simple. It's the one and only question: "How many * (*enter the musician of your choice) does it take to change a lightbulb?" Here are some of the results.

How many drummers does it take to change a lightbulb?
None. They have machines to do that now.

How many drummers does it take to change a lightbulb?
Five. One to change it, and the other four to stand around and talk about how much better Dave Weckl would have done it!

How many drummers does it take to change a lightbulb?
Only one; he holds the bulb and the world revolves around him.

How many drummers does it take to change a lightbulb?
Just one, so long as a roadie gets the ladder, sets it up and puts the bulb in the socket for him.

How many drummers does it take to change a lightbulb?
One, but only after asking, "Why?"

How many bass players does it take to change a lightbulb?
1...5...1, 1...4...5...5...1.

How many clarinetists does it take to change a lightbulb?
Only one, but he'll go through a whole box of bulbs before
he finds just the right one.

How many English horn players does it take to change a
lightbulb?
One, but he gyrates so much, he'll fall off the ladder.

How many French horn players does it take to change a lightbulb?
Just one, but he'll spend two hours checking the bulb for alignment and leaks.

In the 22nd century, how many guitarists will it take to replace a light source?
Five. One to actually do it, and four to reminisce about how much better the old tubes were.

How many oboists does it take to change a lightbulb?
One. But by the time he gets done shaving the tip, you won't need it.

How many sax players does it take to change a lightbulb?
Five. One to change it and four to contemplate how David Sanborn would've done it.

How many second violinists does it take to change a light-bulb?
None. They can't get up that high.

How many trumpet players does it take to change a light-bulb?
Five. One to handle the bulb and four to tell him how much better they could have done it.

How many drummers does it take to change a lightbulb?
1. "Why? Oh, wow! Is it like dark, man?"
2. Only one, but he'll break ten bulbs before figuring out that they can't just be pushed in.
3. Two: one to hold the bulb, and one to turn his throne (but only after they figure out that you have to turn the bulb.

How many sopranos does it take to change a lightbulb?
Two. One to hold the diet cola and the other to get her accompanist to do it.

How many altos does it take to change a lightbulb?
Two. One to screw it in and the other to say, "Isn't that a little high for you?"

How many basses does it take to change a lightbulb?
None. They're so macho they prefer to walk in the dark and bang their shins.

How many tenors does it take to change a lightbulb?
Four. One to change the bulb and three to bitch that they could have done it if they had the high notes.

How many bass players does it take to change a lightbulb?
1. Don't bother. Just leave it out – no one will notice.
2. One, but the guitarist has to show him how to do it first.
3. Six: one to change it, and the other five to fight off the lead guitarists who are hogging the light.

How many country & western singers does it take to change a lightbulb?
Three. One to change the bulb and two to write a song about the old one.

How many sound men does it take to change a lightbulb?
1. "One, two, three, one, two, three..."
2. "Hey man, I just do sound."
3. One. Upon finding no replacement, he takes the original apart, repairs it with a chewing gum wrapper and duct tape, changes the screw mount to a bayonet mount, finds an appropriate patch cable, and re-installs the bulb fifty feet from where it should have been, to the satisfaction of the rest of the band.

How many Deadheads does it take to change a lightbulb?
12,001. One to change it, 2,000 to record the event and take pictures of it, and 10,000 to follow it around until it burns out.

How many punk rockers does it take to change a lightbulb?
1. Two. One to change it and the other to eat the old one.
2. Two. One to change it and the other to smash the old one on his forehead.

$\oint$

How many jazz musicians does it take to change a lightbulb?
1. None. Jazz musicians can't afford lightbulbs.
2. "Don't worry about the changes. We'll fake it!"

$\oint$

How many producers does it take to change a lightbulb?
"...hmm...I don't know...what do you think?"

$\oint$

How many bluegrass musicians does it take to change a lightbulb?
Five. One to change it and the other four to complain that it's electric.

$\oint$

How many contrabass clarinetists does it take to change a lightbulb?
All of them.

How many harpists does it take to change a lightbulb?
Four. One to screw in the lightbulb and three to critique her technique.

How many guitarists does it take to change a lightbulb?
None. They just steal someone else's light.

How many guitarists does it take to change a fluorescent tube?
Three. One to change it and the other two to tell him how much better incandescent bulbs are.

How many electric guitar players does it take to change a lightbulb?
Two, but they stand so close to each other you'd swear they were going to kiss.

How many trombone players does it take to change a lightbulb?
Only one, but he'll spend half an hour trying to figure out what position he needs to be in.

How many guitarists does it take to change a lightbulb?
One, but he'll set the old one on fire.

How many trombonists does it take to change a lightbulb?
Only one, but he'll leave a big puddle of spit on the floor underneath him.

How many bass trombonists does it take to change a light-bulb?
Just one, but he'll do it too loudly.

How many tuba players does it take to change a lightbulb?
Ten. One to change it, and nine to congratulate him down at the pub afterwards.

How many drummers does it take to change a lightbulb?
One. But he's got to do it 3 times.

How many organists does it take to change a lightbulb?
Two. One to change the bulb, and one to complain that the switch doesn't have any combination pistons.

How many music critics does it take to change a lightbulb?
Music critics don't know how, but rest assured they'll find something wrong with the way you do it.

How many techno musicians does it take to change a lightbulb?
Ten. The bulb's already been changed, but you need one to turn on the light and nine to go out to eat.

How many mezzosopranos does it take to change a lightbulb?
Who cares!

How many altos does it take to change a lightbulb?
None, because they cannot reach it.

How many tenors does it take to change a lightbulb?
100. One to screw the lightbulb in, and 99 to whine, "It's too high!"

How many conductors does it take to change a lightbulb?
One, but, then again, who's really watching?

How many Notre Dame Marching Band members does it take to change a lightbulb?
225: one to change the bulb, 24 to play the fight song, and 200 to check the university's standings in the national light-bulb-changing polls.

How many guitar players does it take to change a light-bulb?
Eleven. One to do it, and ten to watch him and say, "I can do that faster."
P.S.: But, there is always one who will ask, "Would Stevie Vai do it that way?"

How many conductors does it take to change a lightbulb?
Seven. (Indignant nose upturning) "Of course, I wouldn't expect you to understand."

How many banjo players does it take to change a light-bulb?
Five. One to screw it in and four to complain that Earl wouldn'ta done it thataway.
- OR -
Four to argue about what year it was made.
- OR -
Four to argue about how much it costs.
- OR -
Four to ask what tuning he's using.

How does Ozzy Osbourne change a lightbulb?
First he bites off the old one.

How many bass players does it take to change a lightbulb?
None - they're all too laid back to bother.
- OR -
None, the piano player can do that with his left hand.

What's grey, crispy and hanging from the ceiling?
A drummer trying to change a lightbulb.

Great lies of the music business

- The booking is definite
- Your check's in the mail
- We can fix it in the mix
- The show starts at 8
- My agent will take care of it
- I'm sure it will work
- Your tickets are at the door
- It sounds in tune to me
- Sure, it sounds fine at the back of the hall
- I know your mic is on
- I checked it myself
- The roadie took care of it
- She'll be backstage after the show
- Yes, the spotlight was on you during your solo
- The stage mix sounds just like the program mix
- It's the hottest pickup I could get
- The club will provide the PA and lights
- I really love the band
- We'll have it ready by tonight
- We'll have lunch sometime
- If it breaks, we'll fix it for free
- We'll let you know
- The place was packed
- We'll have you back next week
- Don't worry, you'll be the headliner
- It's on the truck
- My last band had a record deal, but we broke up before recording the album
- Someone will be there early to let you in

- I've only been playing for a year
- I've been playing for 20 years
- We'll have flyers printed tomorrow
- I'm with the band
- The band drinks for free
- You'll get your cut tonight
- We'll supply someone for the door
- You'll have no problem fitting that bass cabinet in the trunk of your car
- There'll be lots of roadies when you get there
- It's totally compatible with your current program
- You'll have plenty of time for a soundcheck
- This is one of Jimi's old Strats
- We'll definitely come to the gig
- You can depend on me

How to sing the blues

- Most blues begin with "woke up this morning."

- "I got a good woman" is a bad way to begin the blues, unless you stick something nasty in the next line: "I got a good woman, with the meanest dog in town..."

- Blues are simple. After you have the first line right, repeat it. Then find something that rhymes. Sort of: Got a good woman with the meanest dog in town.
  Got a good woman with the meanest dog in town.
  He got teeth like Margaret Thatcher.
  and he weighs 500 pounds.

- The blues are not about limitless choice.

- Blues cars are Chevys and Cadillacs. Other acceptable blues transportation: a Greyhound bus or a southbound train. Not acceptable: Beemers, hot air balloons. Walkin' plays a major part in the blues lifestyle, as does fixin' to die.

- You can have the blues in New York City, but not in Queens or Brooklyn. Hard times in Vermont or North Dakota: just a depression. The best places to have the blues are still Chicago, St. Louis and Kansas City.
- The following colors do not belong in the blues:
  violet
  beige
  mauve

- You can't have the blues in an office or mall: the lighting is wrong.

- Good places for the blues:
    The highway (the best: a crossroads)
    The jail house
    An empty bed

- Bad places:
    Ashrams
    Gallery openings
    Wine tastings
    A weekend in the Hamptons

- Do you have a right to sing the blues?

    Yes, if:
        Your first name is a southern state, like Georgia
        You're blind
        You can't be satisfied
        "The man" doesn't like you
    No, if:
        You were once blind, but now can see
        You're deaf
        You have an IRA

- Other blues liquids:
    Wine from a bottle in a sack
    Irish whiskey from a dirty glass
    Muddy water (usually not for drinking)

- Not blues beverages:
    Any mixed drink, or a drink with a little umbrella in it
    Any kosher wine
    Yoo Hoo (all flavors)

- Some names for blues women:
    Sadie
    Big Mama
    Bessie

- Some blues names for men:
    Joe (including "Big", "Old" or "Blind", alone or in any combination, but not "little")
    Willie (Little Willie could work)
    Lightnin'
    Almost anything with "howlin'" in front of it

- Other name possibilities include physical infirmities: blind, cripple, wheezin'; fruit names: lemon, lime; names of presidents: Jefferson, Johnson, Fillmore.

𝄞

Orchestra personnel standards

Conductor
Leaps tall buildings in a single bound.
Is more powerful than a locomotive.
Is faster than a speeding bullet.
Walks on water.
Gives policy to God.

Concertmaster
Leaps short buildings in a single bound.
Is more powerful than a switch engine.
Is just as fast as a speeding bullet.
Walks on water if sea is calm.
Talks with God.

Oboist
Leaps short buildings with a running start and favorable winds.
Is almost as powerful as a switch engine.
Is almost as fast as a speeding bullet.
Walks on water in an indoor swimming pool.
Talks with God if a special request is approved.

Trumpet player
Barely clears a quonset hut.
Loses tug-of-war with a locomotive.
Can fire a speeding bullet.
Swims well.
Is occasionally addressed by God.

Bassoonist
Makes marks high on the wall when trying to clear short buildings.
Is run over by a locomotive.
Can sometimes handle a gun without inflicting self-injury.
Dog-paddles.
Talks to animals.

Second violinist
Runs into buildings.
Recognizes locomotives two times out of three.
Is not issued any ammunition.
Can stay afloat with a life jacket.
Talks to walls, argues with self.

Manager
Falls over doorstep when trying to enter buildings.
Says "Look at the choo-choo."
Plays in mud puddles.
Loses arguments with self.

Horn player
Lifts buildings and walks under them.
Kicks locomotives off the tracks.
Catches speeding bullets in teeth and eats them.
Freezes water with a single glance.
Is God.

Glossary of musical terms commonly misunderstood by country & western musicians with their translated "country" definitions

12-TONE SCALE:	The thing the State Police weigh your tractor trailer truck with
A 440:	The highway that runs around Nashville
ACCIDENTALS:	Wrong notes
AD LIBITUM:	A premiere
AEOLIAN MODE:	How you like mama's cherry pie
AGITATO:	State of mind when your valve sticks
AGNUS DEI:	A famous female church composer
ALLEGRO:	Leg fertilizer
ALTOS:	Not to be confused with "Tom's toes," "Bubba's toes" or "Dori-toes"
ARPEGGIO:	"Ain't he that storybook kid with the big nose that grows?"
AUDITION:	The act of putting oneself under extreme duress to satisfy the sadistic intentions of someone who has already made up his mind
AUGMENTED FIFTH:	A 36-ounce bottle
B DOUBLE FLAT:	An insect that was squashed twice
B FLAT:	A squashed insect
BACH CHORALE:	The place behind the barn where you keep the horses
BAR LINE:	A gathering of people, usually among which may be found a musician or two
BASS:	The things you run around in softball
BASS CLEF:	Where you wind up if you do fall off

BASSOON:	Typical response when asked what you hope to catch, and when
BEAT:	What music students do to each other with their instruments. The down beat is performed on top of the head, while the up beat is struck under the chin
BIG BAND:	When the bar pays enough to bring two banjo players
BOSSA NOVA:	The car your foreman drives
BREVE:	A sustained note when you run out of bow
BREVE:	The time you spend when the line is short
BROKEN CONSORT:	When somebody in the ensemble has to leave and go to the restroom
CADENCE:	When everybody hopes you're going to stop - but you don't
CADENZA:	The heroine in Monteverdi's opera "Frottola"
CADENZA:	That ugly thing your wife always vacuums dog hair off when company comes
CANTUS FIRMUS:	The part you get when you can only play four notes
CELLO:	The proper way to answer the phone
CHROMATIC SCALE:	An instrument for weighing that indicates half-pounds
CHURCH:	That institution largely responsible for the existence of choirs, choirmasters, organs, and organists. It is also to blame for sermons, offertories, and

	other forms of punishment
CHURCH:	The large damp, draft edifice that houses any or all of the above
CLARINET:	Name used on your second daughter if you've already used Betty Jo
CLAUSULA:	Mrs. Santa Claus
CLEF:	Something to jump from before the viola solo
CLEF:	What you try never to fall off of
COLORATURA SOPRANO:	A singer who has great trouble finding the proper note, but who has a wild time hunting for it
CONDUCTOR:	A musician who is adept at following many people at the same time
CONDUCTOR:	The man who punches your ticket to Birmingham
CRESCENDO:	A reminder to the performer that he has been playing too loudly
CROTCHET:	It's like knitting but it's faster
CUT TIME:	Parole
CUT TIME:	When you're going twice as fast as everybody else in the ensemble
DA CAPO AL FINE:	Go back to the beginning, only play it right this time
DA CAPO AL FINE:	I like your hat
DETACHÉ:	An indication that the trombones are to play with their slides removed
DI LASSO:	Popular with Italian cowboys
DIATONIC:	Low-calorie Schweppes
DIMINISHED FIFTH:	An empty bottle of Jack Daniels
DISCHORD:	Not to be confused with "datchord"

DRONE:	The sound of a single monk during an attack of Crotchet
DUCTIA:	A lot of mallards
EMBOUCHURE:	The way you look when you've been playing the krummhorn
ESTAMPIE:	What they put on letters in Quebec
FIRST INVERSION:	Grandpa's battle group at Normandy
GARGLEFINKLEIN:	A tiny recorder played by neums
GLISSANDO:	A technique adopted by string players for difficult runs
GLISSANDO:	Musical equivalent of an epileptic seizure
HALF STEP:	The pace used by a cellist when carrying his instrument
HOCKET:	The thing that fits into a crochet to produce a racket
INTERVAL:	How long it takes you to find the right note. There are three kinds: 1. Major Interval: A long time 2. Minor Interval: A few bars 3. Inverted Interval: When you have to back one bar and try again Inverted interval: when you have to go back a bar and try again
INTONATION:	Singing through one's nose. Considered highly desirable in the Middle Ages
ISORHYTHM:	The individual process of relief when Vire is out of town
ISORHYTHMIC MOTET:	When half of the ensemble got a different edition / xerox than the other half

LAMENTOSO:	With handkerchiefs
LASSO:	The 6th and 5th steps of a descending scale
LAUDA:	The difference between shawms and krummhorns
MAJOR SCALE:	What you say after chasing wild game up a mountain: "Whew! That was a major scale!"
MELODIC MINOR:	Loretta Lynn's singing dad
METRONOME:	A dwarf who lives in the city
MIDDLE C:	The only fruit drink you can afford when food stamps are low
MINNESINGER:	A boy soprano
MINOR THIRD:	Your approximate age and grade at the completion of formal schooling
MUSIC LESSON:	A form of cruel and unusual punishment inflicted upon young children by their parents, and upon teachers by their shrinking bank balances. In such cases, it is a debatable point as to which one is more unbalanced - the bank account or the music teacher
MUSIC:	A complex organizations of sounds that is set down by the composer, incorrectly interpreted by the conductor, who is ignored by the musicians, the result of which is ignored by the audience
MUSICA FICTA:	When you lose your place and have to bluff till you find it again. Also known as faking

NEUMATIC MELISMA: A bronchial disorder caused by hockets

NEUMS: Renaissance midgets

OBOE: An ill wind that nobody blows good

ORDO: The hero in Tolkien's "Lord of the Rings"

PERFECT FIFTH: A full bottle of Jack Daniels

PERFECT PITCH: The smooth coating on a freshly paved road

PIANO TUNER: A person employed to come into the home, rearrange the furniture, and annoy the cat. The tuner's chief purpose is to ascertain the breaking point of the piano's strings

PIANO: A cumbersome piece of furniture found in many homes, where playing it ensures the early departure of unwanted guests

PLAGUE: A collective noun, as in "a plague of conductors."

PORTAMENTO: A foreign country you've always wanted to see

PREPARATORY BEAT: A threat made to singers, i.e., sing, or else....

QUARTER TONE: What most standard pickups can haul

QUAVER: Beginning viol class

RACKETT: Capped reeds class

RELATIVE MAJOR: An uncle in the Marine Corps

REPEAT: What you do until they just expel you

RHYTHMIC DRONE: The sound of many monks suffering with Crotchet

RISOLUTO: Indicates to orchestras that they are to stubbornly maintain the correct tempo, no matter what the conductor tries to do

RITORNELLO: An opera by Verdi

ROTA: An early Italian method of teaching music without score or parts

SANCTA: Clausula's husband

SENZA SORDINO: A term used to remind the player that he forgot to put his mute on a few measures back

SINE PROPRIETATE: Cussing in church

SONATA: What you get from a bad cold or hay fever

STACCATO: How you did all the ceilings in your mobile home

STOPS: Something Bach did not have on his organ

STRING QUARTET: A good violinist, a bad violinist, an ex-violinist, and someone who hates violinists, all getting together to complain about composers

SUBITO PIANO: Indicates an opportunity for some obscure orchestra player to become a soloist

SUPERTONIC: Schweppes

TEMPO: Good choice for a used car

TEMPUS PERFECTUM: A good time was had by all

TIME SIGNATURE: What you need from your boss if you forget to clock in

TRANSPOSITION:	An advanced recorder technique where you change from alto to soprano fingering (or vice-versa) in the middle of a piece
TRANSPOSITION:	The act of moving the relative pitch of a piece of music that is too low for the basses to a point where it is too high for the sopranos
TRANSSECTIONAL:	An alto who moves to the soprano section
TROPE:	A malevolent neum
TUTTI:	A lot of sackbuts
VIBRATO:	Used by singers to hide the fact that they are on the wrong pitch
VIRTUOSO:	A musician with very high morals. (I know one)
WHOLE NOTE:	What's due after failing to pay the mortgage for a year

𝄞